WHICH
witch
IS WHICH?

A Concise Guide to Wiccan
and Neo-Pagan Paths
and Traditions

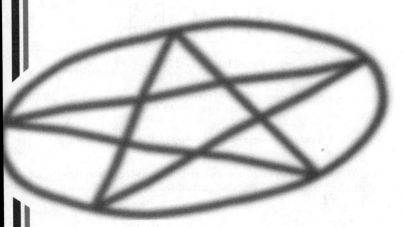

COMPILED AND EDITED BY

PATRICIA TELESCO

New Page Books
A division of The Career Press, Inc.
Franklin Lakes, NJ

WHICH WITCH IS WHICH?
EDITED AND TYPESET BY CLAYTON W. LEADBETTER
Cover design by Lu Rossman/Digi Dog Design
Printed in the U.S.A. by Book-mart Press

To order this title, please call toll-free 1-800-CAREER-1 (NJ and Canada: 201-848-0310) to order using VISA or MasterCard, or for further information on books from Career Press.

The Career Press, Inc., 3 Tice Road, PO Box 687,
Franklin Lakes, NJ 07417
www.careerpress.com
www.newpagebooks.com

Library of Congress Cataloging-in-Publication Data

Which witch is which? : a concise guide to wiccan and neo-pagan paths and traditions / compiled and edited by Patricia Telesco.
    p. cm.
Includes index.
ISBN 1-56414-754-1 (pbk.)
    1. Witchcraft. 2. Neopaganism. 3. Magic. I. Telesco, Patricia, 1960-.

BF1566.T338 2005
299'.94—dc22

                                                          2004048624

NOTE TO
THE READER

In compiling this book, every effort was made to consult with recognized and experienced practitioners within each Tradition or Path discussed. However, this was not always possible, and therefore, where noted, materials should not be construed as "first source." Inevitably, this extensive exploration of Wiccan and Neo-Pagan Traditions, how they're developing and branching out, and to where they're going will grow and change as does the community. Because Neo-Paganism centers on vision-driven Tradition, gentle adaptation, and personal expression, neither the writer nor the publisher of this book can guarantee the total accuracy of the historical and applied information as provided by various contributors.

We also apologize to those Traditions not included, or those whose entries had to be shortened considerably because of page constraints and other limitations. Exclusion, inclusion, and length of entry does not, in any way, indicate preference or superiority. Both writer and publisher acknowledge that there are dozens (if not hundreds) of Paths that we simply couldn't squeeze into this book, and encourage our readers to continue their educational journey beyond this book in wise and creative ways.

ACKNOWLEDGMENTS

With a thankful heart, to the hundreds of people represented in these pages who took time to fill out a survey and share their experiences with me. For one person to try and tackle the diversity of our community would have been impossible. By coming together in this manner, you have helped provide thousands of people with a much more intimate and accurate picture of our beliefs, and helped to celebrate our diversity. Your honest insights and ongoing desire to educate the public in a responsible manner is appreciated tremendously.

Specifically, my respect, admiration, and gratitude to Wren and Fritz at *www.witchvox.com* (and their entire staff), for creating and maintaining the best informational Website in the world! Your never-ending, honorable service to this community serves an example to all of us.

CONTENTS

INTRODUCTION 11

PART ONE: IN THE BEGINNING 15

PATHS AND PRACTICES 21

Solitary or Group Practice 21

Finding a Path 27

Changing Paths 31

**PART TWO: WICCAN
AND NEO-PAGAN GUIDE** 33

TRADITIONS: TRENDS,
TRAINING, AND TENETS 37

"1734" Tradition 37

Adventure Wicca 41

Alexandrian Tradition 44

Appalachian Folk Magick 49

Aquarian Tabernacle Church (ATC) 52

Ár nDraíocht Féin (ADF) 56

Arician Tradition 62

Asatru 66

Avalon Tradition 71

Blue Star Wicca 77

British Druid Order (BDO) 81

Celtic Reconstructionist Paganism (CR) 85

Central Valley Wicca (CVW) 89

Christian Witchcraft 94

Church of All Worlds (CAW) 98

Circle Craft 103

Correllian Nativist Tradition 106

Covenant of Unitarian
Universalist Pagans (CUUPS) 109

Cybeline 111

Dianic Tradition 114

Discordianism-Erisianism 119

Eclectic Wicca and Paganism 123

Esoteric Catholic/Cherokee 128

Faerie Faith 131

Feri Tradition: Vicia Line 134

Gardenarian Tradition 137

Georgian Tradition 141

Golden Dawn 146

Green Witchcraft 149

Gwyddonic Order 153

Haitan Vodou 156

Heathen (Germanic Paganism) 161

Hellenism (Hellenic Ethnic Tradition) 164
Holy Order of Mother Earth (HOME) 166
Keltrian Druidism 170
Kitchen Witchcraft 174
Mahlorian Green Craft 177
Mi'nerwen Tradition 180
Minoan Tradition 184
Mixed Gender Dianic Wicca 187
Mohsian Tradition 190
New England Covens of
Traditionalist Witches (NECTW) 194
New York Welsh Tradition 198
Oak and Stone Path 201
Ophidian Traditional Witchcraft 204
RavenMyst Circle 209
Reclaiming Tradition Witchcraft 212
Roebuck Tradition 217
Santeria/Ifa 221
Seax-Wica 224
Storyteller Wicca Tradition: Thalia Clan 227
Temple of Ara (Ara Tradition) 232
Traditional British Druidry (TBD) 236
Traditional Tantric Tradition 242
Witchcraft 247

INDEX 251

ABOUT TRISH TELESCO 255

Every age, every culture, every custom and tradition has its own character, its own weakness and its own strength, its beauties and cruelties; it accepts certain sufferings as matters of course, puts up patiently with certain evils. Human life is reduced to real suffering, to hell, only when two ages, two cultures and religions overlap.

—Hermann Hesse,
novelist

Is a Bill of Rights a security for [religious liberty]? If there were but one sect in America, a Bill of Rights would be a small protection for liberty.... Freedom derives from a multiplicity of sects, which pervade America, and which is the best and only security for religious liberty in any society. For where there is such a variety of sects, there cannot be a majority of any one sect to oppress and persecute the rest.

—James Madison,
former U.S. President

INTRODUCTION

*Tradition simply means that we need
to end what began well and continue
what is worth continuing.*
——José Bergamín

After a person decides that a metaphysical lifestyle is, indeed, the focus he or she wishes to pursue spiritually, there are a dozen other questions yet to be answered. Among them is determining in which Tradition (if any) he or she will participate. *Which Witch Is Which?* seeks to help people answer this question. How? By giving you an insider's look at various Neo-Pagan and magickal Paths, and by providing you with good analytical tools to ponder those Paths in terms of your day-to-day reality.

Sounds a lot like herding cats to get that kind of collaborative information organized into a book, doesn't it? That's what I thought too. After all, Neo-Pagans have been staunch defenders of independent, creative thought. There was no way to know what kind of response would come from the survey kindly announced by the folks at *www.witchvox.com*.

11

Thankfully, hundreds of practitioners came forward with helpful and very enlightening materials.

From well-known elders, facilitators, and teachers, to solitary eclectics practicing in places as far away as Singapore, it would seem that this subject is near and dear to seekers' hearts. And as I believe you will see in reading, we're not all as different, down deep, as one might expect. I find this both delightful and comforting—we have points of commonality that can draw us together in strength and surety (to me, religion *should* bring people together, not push them apart).

I remember 20-plus years ago when I was introduced to a wide variety of metaphysical practices. While far different than the church of my youth, there was an undefined "something" that appealed to me. I couldn't quite put my finger on it, but I knew I wanted to venture forward and see what was just around the next bend. Unfortunately, at that juncture, there were very few books on New Age religions, and as far as I know, none but Margo Adler's *Drawing Down the Moon* even attempted to examine various Traditions with much more than a brief paragraph or two, unless it was a whole book focused on one approach, such as Starhawk's *Spiral Dance*.

While both these books continue to be of great service to the community, they barely scratched the surface of what has developed since Neo-Pagan Traditions hit the mainstream. Hmm, perhaps saying *mainstreams* is more accurate, considering the sheer volume of variations we have to consider. That's where this book comes in. *Which Witch Is Which?* will become your informal tour guide to the history, beliefs, and practices of many popular Wiccan and Neo-Pagan schools of thought.

Let me back up for a minute. Just as Christianity has many sects, Wiccan and Neo-Pagan practitioners have similar subdivisions. The only real difference here is that we have more branches growing off the tree trunk broadly labeled "New Age Traditions." This rather large umbrella has been opened over everything from Shamanism and Buddhism to Dianic Wicca and Folk magick! Needless to say, that alone can make trying to find just the right Path a little daunting. *New Age* is just too general a term, applied to too many things in today's marketplace.

Wicca and Neo-Paganism narrow the field a little, but even so, you're still looking at literally hundreds of practicing options. Why? Because these approaches to religion stress personal vision and meaningful adaptation as part of their entire philosophy. That means, logistically, there could be as many schools of Wicca and Neo-Paganism as there are people practicing these arts. As one can imagine, all this diversity gets a bit confusing for those trying to understand New Age Traditions, let alone those who have already begun exploring them!

And the confusion doesn't end there. Once you find a Tradition that appeals to your heart and higher senses, there's still the question of whether you'll practice alone or with a group, and if with a group, exactly what group would be best for you. Where exactly does one begin? *Which Witch Is Witch?* offers at least one answer to that question—right here!

From pondering whether to practice alone or with a group to learning all about everything that's available to you, this book becomes a helpmate in the journey. Whether you're just starting out in the Craft or finding that the Path you're on just doesn't seem to fit anymore, there's plenty of information here to at least begin moving in a positive direction. Additionally, you'll find some sound guidelines on potentially mixing Traditions, on contacting groups in which you're interested, and at last, in making those difficult spiritual choices about when and why to involve yourself in *any* Tradition. We've got a lot of ground to cover, so let's get started!

PART one:
IN THE
BEGINNING

> *Both magic and religion are based strictly*
> *on mythological tradition, and they also*
> *both exist in the atmosphere of the miracu-*
> *lous, in a constant revelation of their*
> *wonder-working power. They both are*
> *surrounded by taboos and observances*
> *which mark off their acts from those of the*
> *profane world.*
>
> —Bronislaw Malinowski

Let's assume for a moment you're at the very beginning of exploring what Neo-Paganism (in its broadest
sense) is all about. You're either curious because friends
and family are already involved and you want to know
more about these Pagans and Witches that are appearing
in the media more and more frequently, or perhaps you,
alongside thousands of others, are taking the first steps
in a spiritual journey—you're just starting to sort out
your feelings and consider various metaphysical beliefs
and practices.

No matter what your situation is, you're about to discover the meaning in a very old occult symbol—the Fool
of the tarot. The Fool is on a journey, but isn't "foolish"
in the traditional sense of the word. Art depicts the Fool
standing on the edge of a cliff, with the sun shining and a
happy dog barking at his or her feet. In this moment,
there is no tomorrow, no yesterday, only the *now* and *not
now* that stands between the seeker and discovery. Just
like the abyss—goals, opinions, and ideals lie swirling
before this person with one word at the heart of the activity: *choice*. In this in-between moment, the Fool stops
and breathes—breathes in and centers his or her being,
releases what isn't needed, trusts the First Cause, then
takes the plunge toward discovery. If you're reading this
book, that person is *you*.

When I discovered alternative religions, I was a bit bewildered and overwhelmed by the enormity of energies, ideas, and methods available. So if you're feeling that way, like the Fool before the plunge, don't worry—it's perfectly normal. In fact, truth be told, there are many days when I still feel that way! Wherever my travel takes me, I discover yet another group or approach of which I haven't heard before. Consequently, please realize that this book's ending isn't really written yet, but we're off to a strong running start!

Becuase it's nearly impossible to examine every potential angle in Neo-Paganism, this book has gathered together a buffet, of sorts, for you to sample. Hopefully here you'll find something that suits your tastes and higher senses, something that's meaningful, and something in which you can grow in beauty. No matter what, this exploration is well worth your time. There is no such thing as too much knowledge, too much thought, or too much examination, if it creates a secure, certain foundation from which to understand others, yourself, and your choices.

FOCUS: THE FOOL

Before you begin looking through the rest of this book, consider pausing for a moment and honoring the journey that's brought you to this place of seeking. Something has carried you here, step-by-step, to the cliff of awareness. What is that something? Why are you here? This is no longer about the *hows* of your spiritual practices—focus on the *whys* and let them guide you in the right direction, to the best "right" choice.

The Fool is an archetype for the outset of this new endeavor. In the tarot, this card's number is zero—the number of beginnings and endings, the essence of Spirit, and our intuitive self. In your deepest instincts, you already know what's good for you, what motivates and inspires your humanness to great things. That is your guru, your pilot in knowing what Path of Beauty to take, be it alone or with others.

PATHS AND PRACTICES

SOLITARY OR GROUP PRACTICE

*I am not solitary whilst I read and
write, though nobody is with me. But if
a man would be alone, let him look at
the stars.*

—Ralph Waldo Emerson

Rather than put the cart before the proverbial horse, first take some time and think about whether you prefer to explore alone or find like-minded others with whom to study and work. Both of these options have up sides and down sides, and for the most part, all metaphysical Traditions allow for some leeway in both directions.

It's estimated that the broad-based Neo-Pagan community consists of approximately 70 percent independent (solitary) practitioners. Mind you, New Agers and Neo-Pagans both tend to be an independent lot. We're driven by an inner vision and light that's often hard to explain in words. This makes finding other people who share your exact personal

21

vision relatively difficult, if not nearly impossible. So at least one reason to be a solitary practitioner is that it allows you to stay wholly true to yourself and your inner voice.

A second advantage of the solitary path is not having to rearrange your entire schedule to meet a whole group's convenience timetables. If you're already time-challenged and have a lot on your plate, it becomes difficult to set everything down to go to circle. Yet the people in a group that you join depend on you as part of the energy of the whole. So realizing that your time may not allow for group work is actually a great courtesy. The group won't be left with a gap, and you won't feel bad about breaking a commitment.

For individuals who don't like dealing with group dynamics, the solitary Path affords slightly different advantages. On your own, you need not worry about who's dating who, why so-and-so missed a meeting, and children or pets randomly interrupting circle (unless they're your own!). Perhaps that sounds callous, but it's not—it's simply following the sound rule of "know thyself" and being aware of your tolerance levels.

If you're budget-minded, sometimes the solitary Path is a bit more frugal. Many covens I've interviewed indicate they have specific robes and tools that everyone uses— meaning some type of financial layout. Meanwhile, my robes are whatever I happen to be wearing, and most of my tools come from the kitchen! Note, however, that wise coven leaders have ways to help people get what they need, even if it's a loaner, so this alone should not deter you if you feel really drawn to group work.

Furthermore, if you live in a region or situation where being open about your spiritual beliefs could potentially cause problems (be it with relationships, jobs, or whatever), solitary practice is certainly more private. If you're circling with a group of people regularly, there's a far greater chance that someone will notice or someone in the group will speak about it unwittingly. While I would not wish that anyone had to live "in the broom closet," the reality is that many people still must. Protecting yourself, your means of support, and those your love must ultimately be a primary consideration. As the saying goes, "family first."

The downside of solitary work is that you really have no one but yourself with whom to measure ideas and progress. I know solitary practitioners who find it hard to motivate themselves because they lack consistent contact with other like-minded people to inspire fresh ideas and approaches. The lack of community interaction seems to stall growth, especially with those who enjoy socializing. There are ways to overcome this drawback (like having time set aside for regular self-assessment and goal-making), but humans are tribal creatures. We often *need* other people just for mental health, let alone spiritual well-being.

A coven, grove, study group (or whatever) is like a womb and a safe harbor, if you've chosen one wisely. This group becomes like a miniature classroom in sacred space, apart from the mundane world, where you have no worries about speaking your mind and heart. They are a bit like a spiritual family in which everyone helps make the magick and everyone facilitates each other's growth and transformation.

The kind of communal energy a group can raise is very often substantially greater than one person working alone— that's just basic mathematical reasoning. Additionally, each individual in a group can provide you with unique perspectives on questions, issues, methods, and philosophies with which you may be struggling.

Perhaps the biggest factor that is *pro* group working, to my thinking, is being part of something greater than yourself. When you're in a good circle, where people are really in sync, the ebb and flow of energy is truly amazing. It's timeless, and I've found those moments give me a different sense of my place in the universe than working alone does. It's a wonderful experience.

FINDING SPELL

If you decide that working with a group is best for you, this spell will help you in finding the best one, considering your real-life circumstances and overall mindset. Begin with a small piece of blank paper. Using words or short phrases, describe the type of group you're seeking (such as eclectic, small, politically active, and so on). Fold this paper in on itself three times, saying:

"By the will of one, this spell's begun.
Come the fold of two—the magick is true.
On the fold of three, the magick is free!"

Now wrap the bundle with a long piece of string, leaving enough loose so that you can set the bundle across the table from you while holding the loose end in your hand. Sit down and focus on your intention to find the right group with which to learn and work. Slowly pull on the string so the bundle (the group) moves closer to you. If you'd like to add a verbal component to this part of the spell, simply repeat "come to me," starting out quietly and letting your voice raise naturally with the energy. When the bundle reaches your hand, place it on your altar or in a sacred space. Carry it with you as a charm each time you go to interview a potential group.

In my own life, I have chosen the Solitary Path with periodic open group workings (such as those that take place at Neo-Pagan gatherings and festivals). If it sounds like this approach would also help you, I suggest looking at the book called *Dancing the Fires: A Guide to Neo-Pagan Festivals & Gatherings* by Marian Singer (forthcoming from Kensington Citadel). It not only tells you about hundreds of events, but what you can expect from each.

On the other hand, if you've decided you want to practice with a group regularly, the next obvious question is "How do I find the *right* group for me?" The answer to that question really boils down to the people in any group and how they handle themselves. There are certain situations that should send up a warning flag in your mind, however. These include groups that:

▶ Claim their methods work 100 percent of the time for anyone using them.

▶ Charge unreasonable sums for teaching. (Note: some traditions do have set fees for training, much of which is for materials and so on. There is nothing wrong with asking how the money gets used.)

▶ Have leaders who seem overly controlling or manipulative (the "kiss my ring" types).

▶ Seem to regularly have internal "dramas" that have nothing to do with spiritual practices.

▶ Ask you to overlook a personal taboo or discomfort for the sake of a particular working.

▶ Do not fully and happily disclose your roles, rights, expectations, and responsibilities in that group before joining.

▶ Allow anyone and everyone to join without an interview, trial period, or group consensus (this creates a numbers game—where bigger is definitely *not* better).

▶ Mix and match pantheons or Paths, without much research or understanding of those Beings and customs.

▶ Constantly imply that their approach to magick is the *only* right way.

▶ Read all their rituals and spells (rather than memorizing).

▶ Claim ancient lineage or history, without verification.

▶ Claim any type of certification, training, and so forth, without proper verification and documentation.

▶ Get uppity when you ask pointed, important questions about the group's operation, set up, background, and so on. (Yes, some organizations have information that's only available to people of a certain degree, but the types of questions you'd be asking shouldn't infringe on any vows of confidence.)

▶ Have leaders under the age of 21. (Note: I realize there are some rare teens out there with the maturity, training, and knowledge to run a group, but they are the exception, not the rule. About the only time I see this point being negated is if the group is *by* teens or youth, *for* teens or youth. Even then, however, adult supervision or guidance is a good idea.)

Really, using common sense is nothing less than necessary in your search for a group. Remember that this is your soul's welfare you're entrusting to other people, to some degree. Similarly, be aware that the group with which you're interviewing must consider you in that light too. They have to feel there's good reason for trust and

respect before opening their hearts and spirits to someone new. Typically this isn't a moment for the "bull in a
china shop" approach to matters. Walk gently and thought-
fully, ask questions, and listen a lot. Let both logic and
intuition guide your decision here.

FINDING A PATH

> *Every path to a new understanding begins
> in confusion.*
>
> —Mason Cooley

> *If one hesitates in his path, let him not
> proceed. Let him respect his doubts, for
> doubts, too, may have some divinity in
> them.*
>
> —Henry David Thoreau

Finding a Path will probably have to come before finding a group, because each group's construct will determine
if it's right for you (or not). If you've taken the solitary
approach, finding a Path helps shape your practices, but it
need not be the immediate goal. In either case, trying to
discern what Tradition, customs, ideals, and methods are
most meaningful and inspiring to you is very important to
your spiritual quest.

If you're just starting out, you may be sitting there
wondering how you can even find traditions and ideals to
consider. After all, it's not like such things are listed in
the local Yellow Pages! Part II of this book will become
a valuable resource in your seeking. But it's only one
part of a larger picture. Stop for a moment and think
back on your life. There are all kinds of experiences and
personal connections that can help you in choosing a
positive spiritual construct.

For example, say your family is of predominantly Greek heritage. Considering a Path or group that focuses on Greek mythology and deities would be meaningful and would celebrate that family tree in a unique way. Or perhaps you've always been fascinated by Native American lore. In this case, you might wish to explore Paths that have Shamanic overtones and practices. If you stop and think for a moment, I bet you can come up with two or three themes, such as these that make you feel hopeful, curious, or excited. The best place to start any spiritual journey is from the threshold of your heart and mind.

Besides personal interests and experiences, ask yourself what you like and dislike about various religions to which you've been exposed. Write them down on a list. This information will become very valuable as you're examining Part II of this book, as well as if and when you go to talk to anyone about a particular school of practice.

Other personal questions to ponder include:

▶ How much time do you have to devote to your Craft? Some metaphysical schools (such as High Magick) require a lot of time and study to become proficient. There's nothing wrong with that, but it could prove discouraging, if you can't give it enough time to see real results.

▶ How much can you afford to spend on tools and books? Every Path has different financial layouts. Kitchen Witchery, for example, is by its nature very budget-minded and costs very little, in that most of your tools are already around the house.

▶ How mobile are you? This question probably won't affect the Path you choose, but it could readily affect whether or not you can work with a group focused on that Path.

▶ How much construct (the black and white outlines) do you need to effectively integrate ideas and methods? Some Paths have many "how to" guidelines. Others, such as Kitchen Witchery, are much less defined (and more spontaneous).

▶ In looking at specific Paths, consider the impression you get from the practitioners. Is that an impression with which you're comfortable for *you*?

▶ Do you prefer formal or informal methods and settings?

▶ When you attend a circle or activity held by people following the Paths that attract you, do you find the energy warm and welcoming or more like itchy static?

▶ Do you require a lot of input in your learning process? If so, is there enough printed material on this particular Tradition to help you educationally? Or is there someone you trust from whom you can learn more?

▶ How public do you wish to be with your spirituality? Some metaphysical schools are far more open and publicly active than others. You'll want to find your comfort zone.

I realize this may seem like a lot, but each of these questions will help you narrow the field of possible Paths until eventually you find just the right one. Now, I should mention that some people create a wholly personal methodology and philosophy by which to live. They do this by gathering bits and pieces from a variety of traditions, taking those things that are most meaningful and inspiring, and gently blending them together. The key word here is *gently*.

The Eclectic practitioner must be respectful of the history and cultures represented by ideals and methods they "borrow." This is not only thoughtful towards the people who are fully immersed in a specific Tradition, but it's also respectful and responsible. If you're going to integrate something into your spiritual life, understanding from where it comes and what it means in that setting is nothing less than vital.

The example I give to students, with regard to this mindful blending, begins with Shamanic traditions. In Global Shamanism, practitioners often turn to animal spirits for insights and aid. My adaptation of this is to sometimes call on animal spirits as guardians of the sacred space. However, I do not ask Bear to guard the North at the same time Fish guards the West. Why? Because Bear might be hungry! Without the understanding that Nature Spirits have similar behaviors in the astral realm (as above, so below), the end result of such placement could be pretty ugly.

Similarly, if we consider mythology as our source for understanding Divine Beings to some degree, it's obvious they don't always "play" nicely together. So randomly calling Beings from different pantheons (let alone the same pantheon) into a sacred space is just asking for trouble, unless you have a way to satiate all of them equally well! I wouldn't want to be in the middle of a resulting tiff any more so than a lightning-bolt laden argument on Mt. Olympus!

This doesn't mean that it's impossible to become a successful Eclectic practitioner. Many people have! It just means that there are slightly different considerations in the process.

CHANGING PATHS

Before moving forward to talking about the various Traditions, I'd like to remind people that choosing a Path is not necessarily a "till death do us part" proposition. You need not commit yourself wholly to a Tradition until you're certain it's right for you, and sometimes you can't know that until you venture down the road a bit. Please, however, be honest with others walking that Path about your hesitations and experimentation. So doing will avoid a lot of potential misunderstanding.

For example, I worked for a year with a Strega High Priest who was kind enough to let me see more about this Tradition firsthand. He knew at the outset of our time together that I might not continue practicing but was looking for a little formality to bring to my very informal approach to magick. That time proved incredibly valuable to me, and I found, at the end of it, that Strega wasn't exactly what I needed, but exposure to it helped me greatly. However, if we hadn't communicated honestly about my desires and expectations before working together, I think you can see how this situation could have ended badly.

Similarly, as your life grows and transforms, you may find the Path you've walked for years suddenly feels old, worn out, un-motivating, or just wrong somehow. At that juncture, it's time to pause and assess where the problems lie and why. The reasons that this can (and does) happen varies individually, but rooting out the problem allows you to either resolve it, or find a new direction that resolves that part of the equation. Ask yourself questions such as:

▶ Am I stalled out motivationally? If that's the case, it may not be the Path, but simply a normal stage in your spiritual progress. Everyone experiences times when it seems like nothing is happening. In fact, such times are important so that your mind and spirit can internalize all that you've learned and begin to put it to work in real life.

▶ Have you discovered something about this Tradition that goes against your personal ideals or taboos? If so, is it something that could be changed while keeping the other constructs in place? Note: if you're working with a group, such changes may be impossible other than on a private level.

▶ Has something happened in your life that's drawn you to another Tradition or method? If so, by all means explore it, but don't toss out the old approach immediately. You may find it's just an infatuation rather than a spiritual love affair!

▶ Have you undergone some personal changes that alter your perspectives of the Path you've been walking? This is perhaps the most common reason for considering a new tact. As we transform, our Paths have to grow with us, or we'll stagnate and loose the magick altogether.

If you'll be leaving a group, that may complicate your transition. As with entering any organization, one's departure should be similarly thoughtful and wise. Find a way to express your reasons so that everyone has closure, and you can maintain friendships, even if the spiritual fellowship is ending. There are times to burn bridges, but if your experience with a specific group has been positive, there's no need to hurt anyone's feelings. People who know and respect you will also respect your spiritual choices and support them.

PART
two:
WICCAN AND
NEO-PAGAN
GUIDE

*All of Western tradition, from the late
bloom of the British Empire right through the
early doom of Vietnam, dictates that you do
something spectacular and irreversible
whenever you find yourself in or whenever
you impose yourself upon a wholly unfamil-
iar situation belonging to somebody else.
Frequently it's your soul or your honor or
your manhood, or democracy itself, at stake.*

—June Jordan

*To keep up even a worthwhile tradition
means vitiating the idea behind it which
must necessarily be in a constant state of
evolution: it is mad to try to express new
feelings in a "mummified" form.*

—Alfred Jarry

This section of the book is set up alphabetically, by the name of the given tradition. Readers, I must again stress that there is always the potential for error in any collective such as this. While everyone has done their best to provide accurate information, the individual nature of Neo-Paganism means that 10 people saying they're of _____ Tradition (fill in the blank with anything you wish) could each practice that tradition 10 slightly different ways, and have 10 different views on how it all works together.

I cannot wholly verify the historical authenticity presented by contributors, nor do I necessarily agree with all the views contained herein. Additionally, this is only a condensed glimpse at some of the many Traditions gathered under the Neo-Pagan umbrella. So please take what you see here as generalizations to which you should bring a sound balance of experience, research, wisdom, and mindfulness. Ultimately, it takes more than one book to decide what you're going to integrate as viable ethical, moral, and philosophical guidelines and methods for your life.

Additionally, you'll quickly see that the Neo-Pagan community loves the Internet. Many of the resources provided for further research are URLs. These can and do frequently change in the virtual world, with changing services, providers, and life situations. So if you are seeking a Website and get a "cannot be found" reply, try typing the name of the Tradition into your favorite search engine. Say a prayer and see where that information leads you.

Finally, I would like to thank (again) the people who contributed both insights and detailed writings for this section (and for their patience with editing, in particular); without their voices, readers could not see how various Paths develop, change, and most importantly, how individuals and groups apply those Paths in real life. The diversity presented here also gives us a unique chance to celebrate those things that we all honor: the sacredness of life, the wonders of the human spirit, and the drive to be better human beings.

TRADITIONS: TRENDS, TRAINING, AND TENETS

"1734" TRADITION
By Chas S. Clifton

Although he never crossed the Atlantic, a key figure in the British Craft of the 1960s had a broad effect on American Witchcraft in its formative years. His name was Robert Cochrane, Magister of the Clan of Tubal Cain, described by one of his coveners as "perhaps the most powerful and gifted personality to have appeared in modern witchcraft." The writer was none other than the late Doreen Valiente, who joined Cochrane's coven after leaving Gerald Gardner's.

In Britain, Cochrane's form of the Craft was continued by groups including The Regency (which lasted until 1974) and the Clan of Tubal Cain. In North America, however, the connection was at first entirely postal. Cochrane's letters fell like seed on prepared soil, which, in the mid-1960s, was sprouting both new and transplanted forms of Witchcraft. A lot of cross-pollination occurred, mixing new strains with existing occultism and with entirely new Pagan creations.

In Wichita, Kansas, a small group studying folk magic and psychic development became a conduit for Cochrane's Witchcraft. Joe Wilson placed an advertisement in *The Pentagram*'s final issue seeking contacts, and Robert Cochrane responded, asking his own questions about the existence of "ley lines" in North America and if Wilson understood "the order of 1734." Wilson and Cochrane never were to meet; however, Wilson was able to meet several of Cochrane's former coveners.

In the last six months of his life, Cochrane kept up a brisk correspondence with Wilson, for he had decided that the American had "a deep interest in the faith." He offered many insights into his view of the Craft—one that was more mystical than theological. Like many ancient philosophers, Cochrane saw that even the Gods themselves were subject to Fate, "the single name of all Gods." And unlike many modern Witches, Cochrane was not particularly hostile to Christianity but rather saw the story of the Divine Son and his Mother as a different version of his own Old Religion.

Cochrane described his own Tradition as hereditary, more a *clan* or a *people* than a series of initiates, but one of his letters to Wilson gave his Tradition the name it would carry in North America—the 1734 Tradition—which was "not the date of an event, but a grouping of numerals that mean something to a 'witch.'"

The history of "1734" in North America is complicated, therefore, because it was one of several intermingled threads. While Cochrane's letters to Joe Wilson conveyed a mystical Pagan teaching, they were short on details of physical ritual, coven organization, and the like. Consequently, the 1734 covens in North America tended to borrow from the larger collection of Craft methods—"Gardnerian" in the loosest sense—casting circles deosil with invocations of the four Quarters, drawing down the Moon, having a

Book of Shadows, and so forth. Years later, Wilson himself would accuse some of them of trying to fit Cochrane's Tradition in to an ill-fitting mold, but it was the only mold available for most.

Two coven leaders from Los Angeles, Dave and Ann Finnin, took the trouble to make three trips to Britain and meet with several of Cochrane's former coveners, including Evan John Jones, beginning in 1982. Some of their students later followed them. They had already formed their own 1734-inspired coven, The Roebuck, which incorporated as a legal church (The Ancient Keltic Church) for tax purposes in California in 1990. The Roebuck and its daughter covens make up one of the larger 1734 groups in the area. Others, however, are not organizationally aligned with The Roebuck, but maintain elements of the 1734 Tradition.

Covens in the 1734 share a sort of "family feeling" and a collection of predilections that characterize them, even though these practices are not unique in and of themselves. One is a preference for ritual working outdoors, in forests, in caves, and on hilltops. This Tradition is more of a Mystery religion and less of a fertility religion than some varieties of Wicca. It has its celebratory aspects, but its purpose is to do more than mark the turning of the wheel. Making a spirit-connection with the Old Ones and finding the path to the Castle of Rebirth are its chief concerns. Doing so requires attention to trance work (using hypnosis, masking, and other methods) and to the kind of poetic reasoning embodied in Robert Graves's *The White Goddess*.

Because you are reading this in a collective book, let me make it clear that there is no "authorized" 1734 Tradition. You do not need to be initiated by someone who was initiated by someone who was...and so on, all the way back—1734 is larger than that. When Cochrane wrote to Joe Wilson and set the process in motion, he was hoping himself to recover a connection to people whom he viewed as descendents of Traditional Witches that had migrated to American and who might still be practicing a similar form of the Craft. He thought that he had clues as to their whereabouts, but he died without ever crossing the Atlantic to find out.

Until now, however, the 1734 family has indeed grown and continues to grow. We never claim to be doing exactly what our ancestors did, and we assume that 50 years from now our practices may change again. It is the nature of the Path, as Joe Wilson once observed, to be reinterpreted by each person and for its core concepts to be reexpressed: "It is an initiation granted by the Mysteries themselves, not by a human lineage." So there is no official Book of Shadows, no "stud book" showing who initiated whom. If you walk this Path, you must first learn to trust yourself. Writers can guide you, but you cross the river alone.

FURTHER READING

members.aol.com/akcroebuck
> Home page of the Ancient Keltic Church, the incorporated group of California covens practicing their version of the Tubal Cain tradition.

www.1734.us/joe.html
> Joe Wilson's 1734 Website.

www.cog.org/wicca/trads/1734.html
> A short history of the 1734 Tradition in North America, written by the late Sandy Kopf, High Priestess of Coven AsheshHekat. This portion of the Covenant of the Goddess Website offers summaries of various Witchcraft Traditions.

www.cyberwitch.com/bowers/
> This site offers texts of articles written by Robert Cochrane for *The Pentagram* and *New Dimensions* in the 1960s, as well as some of his correspondence.

www.cyberwitch.com/wychwood/AsheshHekat/
   Home page to another California-based group of
   covens partially based on Robert Cochrane's teachings.
www.witchvox.com/trads/trad_1734.html

ABOUT THE CONTRIBUTOR

Chas Clifton is the editor of *The Pomegranate*, an international journal of Pagan studies (*www.equinoxpub.com*). He will soon have a book on American Wiccan History available through AltaMira Press Pagan Studies series (*www.csulb.edu/~wgriffin/paganstudies/*).

ADVENTURE WICCA
By Ashleen O'Gaea and Canyondancer

A note from Trish: *I've known Ashleen for several years now and am honored by her participation in this book. Her ongoing educational efforts and prison outreach program is not something just anyone could do responsibly. If anyone reading this book is currently corresponding with Neo-Pagan prisoners, or thinking about it, I highly recommend you contact Ashleen for insights, advice, and potential materials.*

Adventure Wicca was founded in 1989 by Ashleen O'Gaea and Canyondancer. Adventure is an ancient human Tradition that found expression though Campsight Coven, O'Gaea, and Canyondancer, who applied it to Wicca. These two initiated each other to First Degree at Samhain in 1986, after two years of study. 1987 saw the first Beltane Village, at Pueblo Park, New Mexico—2003 was Beltane Village XVII! At Litha of 1987, O'Gaea, Canyondancer, and two other people from the Campsight Coven were among the founders of the Tucson Area Wiccan-Pagan Network (TAWN), also still going strong. Even when "unofficial," they helped to organize TAWN's first Fall Festival at Mabon of 1988. In short, this group has been very active!

Adventure is known and defined by synthesis and innovation. Challenging strictly regulated experience and "establishment" interpretations, it is the nature of Adventure not to decree but to set out from doctrine, convention, and ease, and to make camp in the woods beyond. (One of Adventure's mottos is "Enter the forest where the trees are thickest.") The religion of Wicca provides its thealogy, yet the Adventure Tradition does not govern the details of ritual. There is an Adventure Book of Shadows, yet many rituals and most magics are modified or created especially for the Circle in which they're done.

A principle business of Adventure is the confrontation of the Guardians—not the Watchtowers, who are our companions, but those fears and prejudices that hold our personal power hostage. We like our magic to stand to reason. The shared foundations of Adventure Wicca covens are a brave heart, a hospitable camp, and the urge—no, the calling—to see what's around the next bend, whether we're hiking inner or outer trails.

The key deities are Cerridwen and Llyr, Brigid and Lugh, Diana and Herne as aspects of God and Goddess. We hold that all goddesses are aspects of the Goddess and all gods are aspects of her son and consort. (This is not to say that we don't develop personal relationships with particular aspects.) We tend to use their Anglo-Celtic names, when we get more specific than "Lady" and "Lord" or "Triple Goddess" and "Horned One." I think that makes us "duo-theistic," at least by some reckoning.

Clothing for the group often depends on the occasion. We wear white or black robes, and quite frequently circle in street clothes; Initiations are always skyclad. Adventure Dedicants wear green cords; First Degrees, silver; Seconds, red; and Thirds, blue. Here's a sample activity from our group:

Maypole "Instructions"

*The magic of the Maypole's
in the braiding of the strands:
These ribbons are our futures,
and we hold them in our hands!
The more that we are careless,
the greater life's demands—
Dance badly, you will struggle;
dance well and walk on smoothest sands.
With beauty and with strength,
with power and compassion,
With honor and humility,
reverent dance, in mirthful fashion!
Over and under again and again,
weaving the Web's connections—
Ribbons tight! Keep dancing!
And DO NOT change directions!*

CONTACT

Website: *www.AdventureWicca.com*
E-mail: Contact.Us@AdventureWicca.com
Address: Adventure Wicca
    P.O. Box 35962
    Tucson, AZ 85704-5962

ABOUT THE CONTRIBUTORS

Ashleen O'Gaea has been a public speaker and writer for Wicca since 1986. In 1987 she won the Silver Salamander Award for excellence in Pagan Journalism. The Adventure Tradition of Wicca was declared in the winter of 1989, and at Bride of 1991, Campsight encovened, after years of practicing as a circle. At this juncture O'Gaea and Canyondancer took their Third Degrees.

O'Gaea is the author of numerous books including *The Family Wicca Book, Raising Witches,* and *Celebrating the Seasons of Life.* Campsight Coven twice presented TAWN's open Mabon ritual at Fall Fest, and O'Gaea and Canyondancer have been regular guest speakers at the longest-running "Wicca 101" class in Arizona, organized by British Traditional priest Rick Johnson. They have also been presenters at Lord Don Davis's Liberty Spirit Gatherings. In 2000, O'Gaea helped to found Mother Earth Ministries-ATC, a Neo-Pagan prison ministry based in Tucson, Arizona, for which O'Gaea is the senior Corresponding Priestess, and edits a thrice-yearly newsletter.

ALEXANDRIAN TRADITION
By Jimahl di Fiosa

A note from Trish: *You'll begin to see here where several schools of magick, especially what might be deemed ritual or High Magick, are interconnected, akin to the branches of a very large tree.*

The Alexandrian Tradition is one of the major branches of Wicca today. It is considered to be one of the two most prominent of the British Witchcraft Traditions, the other being Gardnerian. The Alexandrian tradition is descended from Alex and Maxine Sanders. Although it is generally thought that the name of the tradition is derived from "Alex," he once stated that it was named, instead, after Alexandria, the ancient city of learning.

Alex Sanders, who many referred to as "King of the Witches," died in 1988. Along with Gerald Gardner, he remains one of the most imposing influences responsible for the resurgence of the Craft in the 20th century and beyond, into the new millennium. Though Alex lived in England, the Alexandrian tradition has since expanded to include members around the world. In addition to the United Kingdom, Alexandrians can be now found in Australia, Belgium, Germany, the Netherlands, and throughout the United States and Canada. In the United States, large communities of Alexandrians can be located in Massachusetts, Florida, and California, as well as many other states.

Alex Sanders was born in 1926. According to June Johns, author of the biographical *King of the Witches* (a book as controversial now as when it was first published), Alex claimed to be initiated by his grandmother when he was a young boy. Johns goes on to write that Alex also claimed to be a descendant of hereditary Witches dating back the 15th century. These claims to alleged Witchcraft pedigree have been hotly disputed by Craft historians. Frankly, this writer considers such arguments to be purely academic.

Alex first came into public view in the 1960s, when he started his first coven in London. The 1960s were the decade of change and revolution of all varieties, no doubt. Alex and his colorful group of Witches drew attention wherever they traveled. Exactly how Alex's first coven came to fruition (like so many elements of his public and private life) is shrouded in controversy. Some think that Alex was initiated by the Gardnerians and subsequently appropriated a Gardnerian Book of Shadows (book of rituals and spells) before starting his own coven. However it happened, there's no denying that Alex and his wife Maxine were a magnificent High Priest and Priestess. From their first fertile steps, the Alexandrian tradition has branched forward and kept on growing.

The basics tenets of Alexandrian Craft are very similar to the Gardnerian tradition. However, because Alexandrian covens are considered to be autonomous and encouraged to contribute to the basic body of lore passed down from Alex, specific rituals and training techniques may vary from coven to coven, or even between various branches of the Alexandrian family. For example, one coven may exhibit a proclivity toward ceremonial magick, another might have expertise in the working of spells and so on. Generally speaking, the basic practices of the Alexandrian tradition include, but are not limited to, the worship of both a God and Goddess, a sincere and unapologetic belief in magick of all types, the awareness of the unseen spirit world, a working relationship with the Elemental forces of Nature, the effectiveness of spells, the transformative power of ritual, and perhaps most importantly, the acceptance of personal responsibility—especially concerning the use of occult power. Or to simplify, each Witch accepts individual responsibility for using his or her powers ethically.

The rituals of the Alexandrian Tradition are enacted within a consecrated magick Circle. The rites are usually officiated by a High Priest or High Priestess, or both. Alexandrian covens may consist of an unlimited number of Witches. They may have as few as three (two coven leaders and one other member) or as many members as the group feels is appropriate. Contrary to popular belief, a coven does not have to consist of 13 members in order to maintain its effectiveness. In larger Alexandrian communities, multiple covens may operate autonomously and yet, at the same time, be under the watchful eye of a Witch Queen whose role is that of a benevolent monarch.

With regard to formal training within an Alexandrian coven, a three-degree system is utilized (First, Second, Third). Many groups also include a preliminary phase in which the postulant is referred to as a Dedicant or Neophyte. One may progress through the degree system by initiation by a properly initiated Witch of equal or greater degree and of the opposite sex. The belief that a Priest can be initiated only by a Priestess and vice versa is a common one in many traditional Paths. It is thought that the basis of this belief lies in the mystery of polarity between the two genders. Some Alexandrian covens have relaxed this requirement, and allow same sex initiations, under specific circumstances.

The final characteristic of Alexandrian tradition is in the use of a Book of Shadows. The Book of Shadows is a handwritten text of ritual lore that is passed from teacher to student. Because the student copies his or her teacher's Book of Shadows by hand (post-initiation), there may be many differences in the content of these ritual texts. The existence of a Book of Shadows is considered by many to be a benchmark of traditional Witchcraft.

Alexandrians utilize many of the traditional tools of Witchcraft. These tools, collected and maintained by each Witch as they progress upward through their education, include a ritual sword (generally used for circle casting and the demarcation of magickal boundaries), a ritual broom which is used to cleanse and purify ritual space, an athame or Witch's blade (considered to be the primary tool of any Witch and one that is necessary to channel the Witch's will in a magickal context), a censer or cauldron for incense, and a chalice (believed to represent the womb of creation). Like many traditionalists, Alexandrians often choose to work skyclad (nude). This lack of attire is usually necessary for the complex initiation rituals. Ritual robes are usually encouraged for the more festive, seasonal celebrations.

To summarize, the Alexandrian Path is one that welcomes any sincere seeker. Although its roots are well anchored in the memory and legacy of Alex Sanders, it is also a Tradition that is as alive and fresh in the 21st century as one could ever hope. Like the mythical Prometheus, Alex delivered the first flame of inspiration to a whole new audience of believers. It is a flame still burning brightly today, passed from one hand to another, guarded diligently, until it has become a light that has spanned the globe.

FURTHER READING

Keepers of the Flame by Morganna Davies and Aradia Lynch

A Voice in the Forest: Spirit Conversations with Alex Sanders by Jimahl di Fiosa

Witches: True Encounters with Wicca, Wizards, Covens, Cults and Magick by Hans Holzer

The Witches' Way by Janet and Stewart Farrar

home.earthlink.net/~jimahl
    Jimahl di Fiosa's personal Website.

www.nectw.org/keepersoftheflame
    Information on traditional Wiccan Paths.

www.starkindler.org
    General information on the Alexandrian Tradition.

ABOUT THE CONTRIBUTOR

Jimahl di Fiosa currently resides near Boston with his two familiars, Luna and Storm. His interest in the occult spans many years. Having been initiated into the Alexandrian Tradition of Witchcraft 16 years ago, Jimahl considers that experience to be a major turning point in his life. Since then, he has devoted his spiritual Path to exploring the mysteries of the Goddess and to the preservation of the Craft for future generations. Areas of special interest include spiritualism, tarot, and ceremonial magick. He also has a strong connection to the folklore and mystery of the Maya. Jimahl is the author of the critically acclaimed book *A Voice in the Forest, Spirit Conversations with Alex Sanders*.

APPALACHIAN FOLK MAGICK
By Ginger Strivelli

> A note from Trish: *If you find that Appalachian Folk Magick appeals to you, you may also wish to check out Paths such as Kitchen Witchery and Green Magick, both of which have similar ambiance and outlooks.*

Not a formal Tradition, the folkways used on this Path came over with Irish and Scottish colonists and blended with the Cherokee native magick and medicine to form the Appalachian Folk magick ways. (Although bits and pieces of African Traditions came to the mountain folks by way of the slaves and bits of Greek/Roman came over with the Scottish and Irish colonists too, it is quite an eclectic Tradition, based mostly in the beliefs of Scottish Irish and Cherokee ancestors.)

To explain, in the 1700s (Common Era) the mass migration of Scottish and Irish people into the southern Appalachians began. The Tsalagi (*Cherokee*, in English) tribe in the area had been there already for hundreds of years at least. The three different magickal Traditions blended, over time, into one modern Tradition of Witchcraft religion and folkways.

The folkways and beliefs were very resilient, as they persisted even in Christian Appalachian families until modern times, in the form of folk remedies, superstitions, charms, and the like. The remaining "Water Witches" and

"Witch Doctors" were almost lost, as modern culture came into the secluded Appalachian Mountains. Even to this day only small pockets of the traditional old Cultural Water Witch and/or Witch Doctor families remain. Very little has been written about this branch of the Witchcraft religion, but for E. McCoy's book *Mountain Magick*. Various old books about the Appalachian culture are the best resources of the Tradition. They include the Foxfire books, the old Farmers Almanacs, the Jack Tales books, and of course the few Cherokee magickal and religious books that have, of late, been published.

In talking about beliefs put into practice, Appalachian Folk are not known for their blind forgiveness; we tend to hold grudges and banish our enemies from our lives, more so than we selflessly forgive and re-embrace those who have wronged us. The ethic of "doing good" is upheld as the most important work one can do, to help one's neighbors and family at all costs—and even helping a stranger is prescribed, unless and until the stranger proves unworthy of such kindness. Animals, plants, and the spirits of Nature are also catered to magically and religiously as a rule of thumb.

Most Appalachian Witches, both now and in the past, have made regular offerings to the "wee folk" (*Yunwi Tsunsdi*, in Cherokee, meaning "the little people," or also still called by the terms used in Ireland and Scotland by our ancestors: *elves, fairies, gnomes*, and so on). Such offerings and magickal work were and are also lavished upon the spirits of Nature, such as dryads, sprites, the winds, the rain, the Father Sun, and the Mother Earth. Most every cake, loaf of bread, or pan of corn bread baked is blessed by throwing a pinch outside for the wee folk and the spirits of Nature.

The Nature Gods are most often worshipped in our Tradition, including the Holly King, Jack Frost/Jack-in-the-Green, Mother Nature/Mother Earth, and Father Sun, the Celtic Gods of our Scottish and Irish ancestors, such as Ceridwen, Kernunnos, Danu, Brigit; and also the

Cherokee Gods of our Tsalagi ancestors, such as Selu (the Corn Mother), Kanati (the Hunter), and Kanene Ski Amai Yehi (Spider Grandmother). Various Greek/Roman Gods are also honored at times, as our ancestors from the Old World had been introduced to the Greek and Roman gods before coming to the New World. Also an occasional African God or Goddess will be mentioned, as those Gods came to us with the slaves from Africa. It is most accurate to say we are quite polytheistic, having many different gods and goddesses with whom we work with and for, though primarily the Celtic and Cherokee deities of our ancestors.

The beauty of this Tradition is that it's a folkway of life. It would be impractical for us to don certain clothing before every spell or rite, as we do multiple rites, spells, and charms a day. It is not a ritualized form of "High Magick," but a true way of life—folk magick in daily use. Altars are common, though, and often made out of the traditional Appalachian folk crafts, such as twisted stick tables and chairs, braided rag rugs, quilts, dream catchers, whittled items, baskets, brooms, ceramic pots, and skins and hides. Magickal tools are also commonly used, including most notably the dowsing rod or *wand*.

To give you an example of our approach, what we call *Haints* are widely feared as angry ancestral spirits, and many spells, charms, and rituals are practiced to keep these troublemakers at bay. One of the most interesting and common Haint related spells requires that the doors of a home be painted "Haint Blue." Haint Blue is a bright baby blue with a periwinkle tinge, very close to, but about one shade darker than, the Carolina Tarheels' blue color. This color is believed to repel the spirits and keep them out of the home. It is most commonly used as the color of a door, but one will often see windows, porches, whole houses, and various items painted that color, to ward off evil spirits and energy when an Appalachian Witch fears negative influence from the spirit world is hounding him or her.

FURTHER READING

The Jack Tales by Richard Chase
Mountain Magick by Edain McCoy
Myths of the Cherokee by James Mooney
Scottish Witchcraft by Raymond Buckland
Voices of Our Ancestors by Dhyani Ywahoo
www.angelfire.com/nb/appalachianpagan
    Appalachian Pagan Alliance Website.
www.witchvox.com/trads/trad_afmt.html

ABOUT THE CONTRIBUTOR

Ginger Strivelli is the cofounding and leading priest-ess of the Appalachian Pagan Alliance (*www.angelfire.com/nb/appalachianpagan*). Ginger is also currently the national president of Pagan Unity Campaign, or PUC (*www.paganunitycampaign.org*), and serves as the North Carolina state chair for the Alliance of Pagan Voters. She has been a writer for Circle Network Magazine during the last 10 years. Many of her articles appear on *www.witchvox.com* and various other Websites and in a number of religious publications.

AQUARIAN TABERNACLE CHURCH (ATC)
By Peter Pathfinder Davis

A note from Trish: *Peter Pathfinder Davis has been one of the trailblazers for Neo-Pagan practitioners. He was one of the first to help me in my early years with some sound advice and insights. The beauty of the ATC is that it, like its founder, embraces diversity and encourages positive creativity as essential to the human spirit.*

The Aquarian Tabernacle Church, is the creation of Pete Pathfinder Davis, who serves as Archpriest, along with Deborah K. Hudson, who is Archpriestess of the Tradition worldwide. ATC is based on English Traditional Wicca, with a focus of serving the larger Pagan communities by providing open worship opportunities to the public, education, interfaith liaison, and in general, providing the infrastructure available to the followers of most faiths but previously just not available to Wiccans and Pagans— things such as major Sabbat festivals, full and new moon worship, a place to gather, a lending library, and many other services associated with faith communities.

This all started on October 31 of 1979, when Pete and a few friends decided to form a formal church organization and established the ATC. It was their intention to establish a quiet place in the countryside outside of Seattle, where Wiccans and Pagans could gather for worship without being hassled by ignorant neighbors or suspicious authorities who did not understand their benevolent nature-worship practices. With the participation of many like-minded Pagans, the ATC grew and flourished.

The ATC is a hierarchic organization, though you'd seldom notice that from the way things are done. There is a large core group of about 40 people who are deeply immersed in the activities, outreaches, and events of the church, and an overall membership in the Pacific Northwest of in excess of 300. The Archpriestess and Archpriest oversee the overall activities of the church, both locally and on an international basis. Virtually all decisions are arrived at through discussion and compromise, in the best interests of the mission of the church, by consensus. Rarely, if ever, has a vote been taken on anything. The Archpriesthood, however, retains the right of veto if they believe an action is not, in the long run, going to be in the best interests of the church or Paganism in general.

To be ATC clergy, one must complete a four-year college-level seminary program, culminating in the award of a Bachelor of Ministry degree from Woolston-Steen Theological Seminary, with recognized religious education status by the Washingotn Higher Education Coordinating Board. The Seminary also has Masters and Doctorate programs available. ATC does not intend to try to tell anyone how they should conduct their own clergy training, but we are fully committed to the professionalization of the clergy of our own Tradition, if they are to undertake matters as serious and delicate as pastoral counseling in the areas of life strategies, marital problems, and psychological and childhood trauma.

This is just a basic outline of the ATC's history and accomplishments. Noted author Raymond Buckland, the man credited with bringing Gardnerian Wicca to the shores of the United States, has said "the ATC has grown by leaps and bounds to become one of the most respected Wiccan institutions in the country, if not the world."

This is illustrated by several notable moments in our history. For example, in October of 2001, the first outdoor circle of tall standing stones was erected within the confines of the Twin Rivers Correctional Facility, as a place of Wiccan worship. To our knowledge, there exists no other state-sanctioned Wiccan outdoor stone circle intended for inmate worship anywhere in the world.

On April 2, 2001, ATC formally incorporated a young people's nature lore and woodcraft program, because of the demand for some alternative to the Boy Scouts. SpiralScouts was launched as an international organization. SpiralScouts (note, it is one word) was developed through an online committee of slightly more than 500 participants, presaging its phenomenal acceptance and growth in the Pagan community worldwide. The program is adaptable to any nonhostile religious community. As of January 2002, there were more than 40 chartered SpiralScouts groups in the United States and Canada. The program continues to grow rapidly. (See *www.SpiralScouts.org*.)

CONTACT

Website: *www.aquatabch.org*
E-mail: ATC@AquaTabCh.org
Phone: (360) 793-1945
Fax: (360) 793-3537
Address: ATC
 48631 River Park Drive
 P. O. Box 409
 Index, Washington 98256

ABOUT THE CONTRIBUTOR

(The Rt. Rev.) Peter Pathfinder Davis is the Archpriest of the Aquarian Tabernacle Church. While he discovered Paganism in his teens, at the age of 50, he was able to retire and pursue his ministry.

Pete served in 1983 as the first Public Information Officer and official spokesman for the Covenant of the Goddess, an international association of Wiccan churches based in Berkeley, California, and was responsible for issuing the group's first public information "press packet," much of which is still in use today. He is a published author and has served as an Adjunct Professor of Religious Studies, teaching basic courses on the Wiccan religion at area colleges.

Pete recently completed two terms as the elected president of the Interfaith Council of Washington, and presently serves as a member of the ICOW Executive Committee. He also is the official Wiccan advisor to the Washington State Department of Corrections Religious

Program and a member of the department's Religious Advisory Commission, overseeing the institutional religious programs under appointment by the state secretary of corrections. He is the author of the sections on Wicca in the *Washington Department of Corrections Manual on Religious Beliefs and Practices* (original and revised editions).

ÁR NDRAÍOCHT FÉIN (ADF): A DRUID FELLOWSHIP, INC.
By KiaMarie Wolfe

A note from Trish: *My personal experiences with ADF leads me to say that they are among the most professional group with which I've ever come in contact. Requests for information are met with timely and numerous replies, even from the very busy leadership. I tip my hat to you!*

The original Druids are dead and gone. They disappeared into antiquity centuries ago and left no recorded accounts of their practices and beliefs. Fragments of their Paleo-Pagan Traditions may have withstood the tests of time, suppression, and assimilation, but what was passed down was a far cry from the truths of their era. Like many ancient mores, the Druid way of life was near the brink of extinction. Some tried to revive the old Traditions, basing their views on romanticized accounts of ancient lore, analysis of fragmentary evidence, and perhaps a few subjective ideas of their own. A plethora of writers and scholars emerged between the late 19th century and the present, each giving his or her theory of what the original Druids did and what we should do to follow in their steps.

In 1983, Philip Emmons "Isaac" Bonewits took the stage, with a plan—and a vision. His vast experiences—as an ordained priest in the Reformed Druids of North America (1968); as founder of the Aquarian Anti-Defamation League (leader 1974–1976); with Ordo Templi Orientis (member 1977–1982); as an ordained Wiccan priest of both the Gardnerian Tradition and New Reformed Orthodox Order of the Golden Dawn; and as an accomplished author of the books *Real Magic* (1971), *The Druid Chronicles Evolved* (editor and coauthor, 1974), and *Authentic Thaumaturgy* (1978)—elevated him to such a station that, when he spoke, people listened.

Isaac's plan was to research, substantiate, and reconstruct the cultural foundations, customs, and polytheistic practices of the ancient Indo-Europeans through sound scholarship and combine that with the well-founded Neo-Pagan Traditions that have developed over the last century. The result would be an in-depth modern form of Druidry that would be both applicable to our own spiritual endeavors and honorable to the ancient Druids from whom it was derived—a revival of the most revered qualities of the Paleo-Pagan (original) faith of our predecessors within a nondogmatic, pluralistic, and scientific framework. His vision saw a contemporary credo dedicated to excellence—intellectually, spiritually, artistically, and physically—whose potential was as far-reaching as the stars. Furthermore, his vision was of a publicly available religion, bringing the long hidden mysteries out of the darkness and making them available to everyone to integrate into their lives and to pass on to their children. With the help and support of a handful of independent scholars, Ár nDraíocht Féin was born! Since its inception in 1983, ADF has grown into one of the largest and most widely spread Neo-Pagan Druid organizations in the world. We are a very organized and respected tradition, and offer a wealth of opportunities for learning and worship.

Ár nDraíocht Féin (pronounced *arn ree-ocht fane*) means "Our Own Druidism" in Modern Irish. Although the name is Gaelic, it should be noted that ADF is not exclusively Celtic or Irish. We seek to acknowledge and celebrate the similarities and variations within the entire Indo-European language group: Celtic, Norse, Slavic, Baltic, Hellenic, Greek, Roman, Vedic, Latin, and other Indo-European peoples. Through recognition and commemoration of the Kindreds (Nature Sprits, Ancestors, and Shining Ones—Gods and Goddesses), we revere the Earth and all life upon it, as well as the Divine Spark within each one of us. This spirituality manifests itself through ecological awareness, scholarly excellence, liturgical training, artistic expression, psychic development, alternative healing and therapy, and more. We work together to fashion magical and religious rites that are relevant in a current context while, at the same time, breathing new life into the Traditions of our predecessors, thus engendering profound change within ourselves and the world around us. As new information becomes available through archaeological evidence and the elucidation of ancient manuscripts and historical documentation, the precepts governing ADF will continue to grow and develop.

ADF, recognized by the IRS as a 501(c)3 nonprofit corporation registered in the state of Delaware, is an open membership organization. Joining consists of filling out a confidential membership form and sending in very affordable yearly dues. It should be noted that an individual does not need to be of Indo-European descent to be a member of ADF. Contrary to a popular misconception that the ancient Druids were an exclusive group of patriarchs, both men and women are welcome. Age, nationality, color, gender, and sexual orientation are irrelevant to participation, and you don't have to be a member to attend our rituals. No one has to abandon other religious beliefs to be a member of ADF, for we strictly adhere to the principle of religious tolerance. There are no secret initiation rituals or leaders with privileged, inaccessible clergy status. As a matter of fact, everyone has the opportunity to study to become a priest. But priest credentials are attained only with a dedicated measure of documented study and application. We offer a number of study programs: the prerequisite Dedicant's Program (which must be completed before taking any other study programs) that covers the basics of Druidry and acts as a foundation for further study; a clergy training program, provided by the Clergy Council, which consists of three circles (levels or courses of study); a Generalist Program; and a number of study programs provided by various guilds. Each study program is essentially equivalent to a bachelor's degree, and each guild has a course of study in place or in process of completion. Only ADF members in good standing may participate in these study programs.

The various guilds have been grouped according to the basic tripartite organization of Indo-European society (as expounded by the scholar, philologist, and cultural historian Georges Dumezil 1898–1986). The three divisions are Divine (magical/religious), Martial, and Economic (producer). The following is a list of guilds currently active: Divine-Bardic Guild (study and training in artistic expression through speech, writing, and song), Liturgists Guild (study and training in the art and science of liturgy, within the context of ADF), Scholars Guild (study and training involving scientific and scholarly research on the roots of ADF), Seers Guild (study and training in the skills of divining, trance work, and counseling), Magicians Guild (study, training, and practice of the traditional arts called *magic*), Martial-Warriors Guild (training in spiritual, mental, and physical defense, and emergency response), and Economic-Artisans Guild (study and training in the making of artworks and crafts), Healers Guild (study and training in a variety of healing arts), and the Naturalists Guild (study and training focusing on the land and the Nature Spirits). Besides study programs, we offer a number of

Special Interest Groups (SIGs) and the Kins, which are culturally specific groups. All in all, there is a wealth of information, study, and additional avenues to express and realize your utmost desires!

Organizational structure starts with the Mother Grove, which consists of an elected governing body with representation encompassing the groups, councils, guilds, and regions. Within each region, semiautonomous groves (groups of individuals meeting within a geographical area) gather together for regular public worship on the eight High Days (solstices, equinoxes, and the halfway points between, known as *fire festivals*), for other rituals deemed appropriate to their cultural background (moon or agricultural observances), and for social sacraments (Rites of Passage, weddings, and so on). As per ADF bylaws, groves are mandated to observe at least the eight seasonal celebrations (known as the Wheel of the Year), file quarterly reports to maintain accurate records of grove activities and finances (IRS requirement), and to observe a standard liturgical outline. Solitaries (individuals worshipping outside of an established group) have access to all of the benefits of membership and a number of e-groups and lists are available to address their specific needs.

Within a standard ADF rite, sacred space is established but not moved beyond the earthly plane. With the help of the Gatekeeper, portals are established which link us to all planes of time and being, and provide conduits by which the Kindreds can communicate and interact with us. The main focus of ritual is praise and offering to those whom we hold in sacred esteem. An omen is received and interpreted after the praise offerings, to elicit a response from the Kindreds, indicating if the gifts were acceptable and to accept any counsel they may have to give us. If the response is favorable, they shower us with ethereal blessings multiplied thousands-fold through a return flow, called *the Waters of Life*. The Waters are showered down upon the participants, into the earth, and caught up in vessels of water, ale, whiskey, hearthstones, or whatever the individual group uses as a medium, depending on the cultural pantheon they embrace. The mediums are shared with the participants and used to perform any magical workings. Besides giving praise and offering, each of the Kindreds is given thanks at the end of the ceremony.

We see divinity within and without, and thereby hold all life to be sacred. We honor our ancestors, the sprits of nature (of which we are a part and not masters over), and a vast array of Gods and Goddesses (none of them being the epitome of ultimate good or evil). We seek excellence in all aspects of our lives but know that, as humans, none of us has all of the answers. With our noses to the grindstone, an ear to the past, an eye on the future, and hands joined in community, we walk together on the Path of the ancients. And so can you.

This article is a compilation of information presented on the ADF Website (*www.adf.org*). For in-depth articles on topics presented, recommended reading, or to find a grove near you, visit the site.

ABOUT THE CONTRIBUTOR

An active Pagan for the past 25-plus years, KiaMarie Wolfe is a former Celtic Faerie High Priestess and has conducted workshops at various Pagan events, covering topics such as Druidry, Wicca, comparative religion, and energy flow in ritual. She is an avid hand drummer and has facilitated numerous drum circles and workshops throughout the Northeast with special emphasis on energy dynamics, group interaction, the healing and therapeutic aspects of drumming, and drumming as a mystical rite. A member of ADF since 1992, she is currently serving her second term as Senior Druid of Muin Mound Grove, ADF, and acts as grove liturgist and bard.

ARICIAN TRADITION
By Raven Grimassi

A note from Trish: *Raven Grimassi was among the first of a growing number of authors to bring some of the older Traditions of the Craft into the public eye. He did so with an awareness that blending history with modern reality isn't easy and that you're bound to take some flack along the way. Nonetheless, he is to be thanked, as efforts such as his ensure that the ancient Mysteries will not be forgotten or forgone.*

The Arician Tradition was founded in 1998 by author Raven Grimassi. It is a blend of modern concepts along with many ancient beliefs and practices that once comprised the religious rites held in the sacred grove of the goddess Diana at Lake Nemi, Italy. The Tradition also incorporates modern adaptations based upon the ancient Mystery Schools of the Aegean/Mediterranean region. The Arician Tradition is an offshoot of the Aridian System, which is a modern Tradition for Americans interested in the Old Religion of Italy. The Arician Tradition is an Initiate System, as opposed to the Aridian System, which only requires self-dedication. Although, as practiced today in its entirety, the Arician Tradition is a modern system, it is based largely upon the archaic beliefs and practices of Old Europe. The Arician Tradition is structured as a European Mystery Tradition, teaching and training individuals in the essential concepts of the Old Religion.

One of the primary tenets of the Arician Tradition is that the Earth is a conscious being, and that every living thing upon the Earth is intimately connected. We believe in reincarnation, both in the material dimension and the spiritual dimensions. We view the soul as a student being trained and educated in each lifetime. Our basic tenets are:

▶ The Source of All Things is both masculine and feminine.

▶ Our souls bear the divine spark of the Creators.

▶ The essence of the Creators is reflected in the Creation.

▶ Nature is the Great Teacher, the microcosm of the Divine Blueprint (as above, so below).

▶ We are spiritual beings having a human experience, and not humans having a spiritual one.

▶ Reincarnation is a process through which the soul is prepared and then liberated.

▶ Our actions, or lack thereof, affect others, and we must strive for peaceful coexistence.

▶ All life forms are equal, for life is life, no matter what container it dwells in.

▶ We are responsible for our own actions, and there are consequences for irresponsibility.

▶ What we do to the Earth and to each other, we do to ourselves.

▶ Nothing may be received without something being given back in return.

▶ We are guided by the deities and spirits that accompany us on our Path.

▶ Love and compassion are essential for a healthy and evolving soul.

▶ Structure and individualism should remain in balance, one not overshadowing the other.

Also central to our beliefs is reliance upon the Mystery Teachings as a path-work leading to enlightenment. The

Primal Mysteries are concerned with the Women's and Men's Mysteries. The Middle Mysteries are focused upon Nature and the inner mechanisms; this level also contains the greater magickal training. The High Mysteries are focused upon Divinity, the goddesses and gods, and how we connect and interact.

We believe that the ancient Mystery Teachings hold the accumulative knowledge and wisdom of our ancestors. We refer to this as the "well-worn path" and we value it as the sum perspective of the multitude of people who lived and practiced the ways, long before we embraced them. As part of the Mystery Teachings, we acknowledge the forces of Light and Darkness, which are the forces of gain and decline. To us, there are blessings in both types of energy.

In the Arician Tradition, we believe that the "witches of old" were actually the priests and priestesses of an old European Mystery sect that evolved over the ages, gathering the people and directing them in celebratory rites. In the modern Arician Tradition, the clergy are divided into two categories: priest/priestess and High Priest/High Priestess. The role of the priest or priestess is to be available to council and assist the initiated members as requested or needed. The duties of a priest or priestess also include maintaining a personal shrine, conducting rituals, teaching the ways, and initiating others into the Craft. They may also perform the community rites of birth, marriage, and death.

The role of the High Priestess or Priest is to teach and train those who will comprise the Priesthood/Priestesshood. Understanding and conveying the Mystery Tradition is the special focus of the High Priesthood or Priesthood. The High Priest or Priestess directs the eight Sabbat gatherings during the year, as well as the full moon rites. He or she is typically the figure who handles matters of public education and awareness.

In terms of organization, the Arician Tradition is comprised of individual covens. Our word for a coven is a *boschetto* (pronounced *boss-ket-toe*) meaning "a grove of trees." A coven can be comprised of three to 13 people, and can hive off to form new covens. A Grand Council of Elders, which represents the Tradition as a whole, guides the covens of the Arician Tradition. Each coven has its own Coven Council of Elders as well as a representative to the Grand Council. An individual known as a *Grimas* guides the Grand Council. The Grimas is the directing Elder of the Tradition itself.

The Tradition is secured for survival into future generations by a code of rules. One of the chief rules, in this regard, is that nothing may be removed from the ways of the Tradition, but that things may be added. This ensures that the system can adapt and grow in new environments, but can also carry with it the traditions, beliefs, and practices that make the Tradition cohesive and defined. Thus the wisdom of our Elders does not become lost, nor do the visions of our youth become buried by the status quo.

The core element of our code of conduct lies in our total acceptance of self-responsibility. We do not believe in forcing our will upon others, and we seek to live in peaceful coexistence. While we do not desire to harm anyone, we do believe in protecting ourselves, as necessary. Ultimately, we strive to live in awareness and compassion concerning those around us, and we seek to live in common cause with Nature. Consequently we venerate Nature and the patterns of Nature in our worship throughout the year.

CONTACT

E-mail: Ravnloft@pacbell.net

FURTHER READING

Ancient Philosophy, Mystery, and Magic by Peter Kingsley

Etruscan Roman Remains by Charles Leland

The Gods and Goddesses of Old Europe by Marija
    Gimbutas

Hereditary Witchcraft by Raven Grimassi

Italian Witchcraft by Raven Grimassi

Italian-American Foklore by Frances M. Malpezzi and
    William M. Clements

The Wiccan Mysteries by Raven Grimassi

*Witchcraft and Magic in Europe: Ancient Greece and
    Rome* by Bengt Ankarloo

Women's Mysteries by Esther Harding

www.stregheria.com/

www.witchvox.com/trads/trad_arician.html

ABOUT THE CONTRIBUTOR

Raven Grimassi is an award-winning author of nine books on Witchcraft and Wicca. He is the Directing Elder of the Arician Tradition and the foremost authority on the works of Charles Leland pertaining to the field of Witchcraft.

ASATRU
By Janna Pereira

Asatru is the modern reconstruction of the religion of the pre-Christian Germanic peoples, an attempt to intelligently recreate those ancient practices in a modern setting, with an emphasis placed on historical research and scholarly interpretation. Practice primarily consists of honoring the gods, goddesses, spirits and other helpful beings within this context.

There are two complementary "tribes" of gods and goddesses in the Germanic cosmology, the *Aesir* and the *Vanir*. One way of looking at them is to say that the Aesir are associated with things human beings do (war, justice, social relationships) and the Vanir are associated with the way human beings interact with the natural world (fertility of land, sexuality, human fertility, luck while fishing).

The exact number of gods and goddesses is somewhat subject to interpretation. Some of the better-known gods are Odin, Thor, Tyr, Balder, Njord, Frey, and Heimdall. Whether Loki (a trickster being that some assign to a powerful spirit but that other see as a deity) is counted among the gods is up to the individual! Among the goddesses, the best known are probably Frigga, Freya, Skathi, Ostara, and Sif.

Germanic cosmology has many beings that are not gods and whose exact nature and role is poorly defined. There are land spirits or house spirits, associated with particular places or houses. There are *jotuns* (also called *giants* or *etins*) who tend to take an oppositional role to humanity and the Gods. There are *alfar* (more commonly translated as *elves*) who seem associated with the powers of fertility or, perhaps, the dead. There are also *disir*, who seem associated with female ancestral spirits.

The presence of so many beings can best be understood by keeping in mind the importance of relationships in Germanic cosmology. If there is bad luck in the household, it wouldn't hurt to ask one's patron deity for help, but it may be more appropriate to make an offering to the local house spirit or even to one's ancestral spirits.

There are Nine Worlds, including the world of humans (Midgard) and the world of Gods (Asgard). The World Tree connects all the Nine Worlds, and binds them together. (The Nine Worlds are Midgard, Asgard, Vanaheim, Jotunheim, Svartalfheim, Alfheim, Nifleheim, Muspelheim, and Hel's Realm.)

The symbol of Asatru is the Thor's Hammer. Modern practitioners of the religion typically wear one around their neck. People might also wear other pieces of jewelry with personal significance, but the Thor's Hammer is the most widely known and recognized symbol of Asatru.

Many Asatruars acknowledge a list of values known as the Nine Noble Virtues. This is a modern list, distilled from the lore and intended to embody certain important concepts within Heathenism. There are different sets of Nine Noble Virtues, but the most common list consists of Courage, Truth, Honor, Fidelity, Discipline, Hospitality, Industriousness, Self-Reliance and Perseverance.

The primary ritual in Asatru, known as the *blot* (long "o" sound, to rhyme with *float*), in its simplest form, consists of an offering, typically of drink. Blots are usually performed to a single deity or group of beings (land spirits, ancestors, honored dead). It would be very unusual to honor a God/Goddess pair as is often done in Wicca.

Despite the very basic form, a blot can become very elaborate and include lengthy invocations to the deities, readings, rune divinations, magical workings, and even dramatic reenactments of the myths.

There is also a drinking ritual known as the *sumbel*. During sumbel, people take turns drinking from a horn (or horns), solemn oaths are made to the gods and witnessed by all participants. It is also common to brag about achievements made since the last sumbel, and thank the Gods for their influence and inspiration. Speech may take a lighthearted turn, and then, just as quickly, turn to more serious matters. The more ambitious may recite poetry or tell stories. Sumbels may be free-form, or each round may have a specific theme.

There are a few historically important holidays that many groups and individuals celebrate, and there is a certain consistency between calendars from different groups.

However, there is no unified "Wheel of the Year," and each holiday calendar tends to reflect the needs of the people involved. Solitary practitioners might even center their practice around honoring specific gods or goddesses and helpful spirits, with minimal emphasis on the seasons.

There are two basic types of magickal practice. The first is the more commonly known *runic* magic, and the second may be loosely described as a Shamanic series of practices known as *seidhr*. A thorough examination of what we know of these magicks and how this translates into modern practice is far beyond the scope of this introduction, but for people inclined towards study and further knowledge, there is much to explore and ponder.

FURTHER READING

Gods and Myths of Northern Europe by Hilda Roderick Ellis Davidson
> This is one of those rare sightings—an academic book written with a poetic sensibility.

Nine Worlds of Seid-Magic by Jenny Blain
> This book explores a series of vaguely Shamanistic practices known as seidh, which are not so well known outside of the Asatru and greater Heathen communities.

Norse Myths, by Kevin Crossley-Holland
> An exceptional modern retelling of the Norse myths. The book is lively, enjoyable, and respectful of the source material. If you're having difficulty getting through the *Prose Edda* or *Poetic Edda*, read this book. There are also extensive notes (about 50 pages worth) at the back, talking about sources and themes and making connections between different myths.

The Poetic Edda (Lee Milton Hollander or Carolyne Larrington translation)

Unlike the *Prose Edda*, we know very little of the history of the *Poetic Edda*. The material within this collection appears to originate from different time periods, but the main manuscript was almost certainly written down by an unknown Icelander writing in the last half of the 13th century. These two very different translations are in print and readily available.

The Prose Edda (Jean Young or Anthony Faulkes translation) by Snorri Sturluson.
Sturlson, an Icelandic statesman who lived between 1179 and 1241 CE, was a scholar and a historian who was concerned about the poetic tradition of Iceland dying as the old stories about the Gods were gradually forgotten. The Prose Edda is a reference that includes both mythological tales and material intended to instruct aspiring poets and, incidentally, preserved a great deal of material of interest to modern Heathens.

Rudiments of Runelore by Stephen Pollington
This is aimed at the dedicated layperson who wishes a scholarly introduction to the runes.

home.earthlink.net/~jordsvin/Seidhr/Index.htm
Jordsvin's Seidhr 101 syllabus.

www.dickinson.edu/~eddyb/mythology/Cover_page.html
Germanic mythology.

www.erichshall.com/asanew/newtotru.htm
Asatru Basics.

www.pitt.edu/~dash/mythlinks.html
Germanic myths, legends, and sagas.

www.sacred-texts.com/neu/index.htm
Sacred texts—legends and sagas (especially the Northern European, Germanic, Icelandic, and Scandinavian sections).

www.sunnyway.com/runes/
Runes, Alphabet of Mystery.

www.thetroth.org/resources/ourtroth
   Our Troth.
www.thorshof.org
   Thorshof.
www.ugcs.caltech.edu/~cherryne/mythology.html
   Norse mythology Web page.
www.webcom.com/~lstead/Ravenbok.html
   Ravenbok.

ABOUT THE CONTRIBUTOR

   Janna Pereira has been Asatru for about 14 years. During that time, she has participated in both Asatru and Neo-Pagan events, attended fests and moots, and been a leading member of Raven Kindred South for several years

AVALON TRADITION
By Jhenah Telyndru

   The Sisterhood of Avalon (SOA) is an International Celtic Women's Mysteries Organization that seeks to balance intuitive wisdom with scholastic achievement. The SOA is composed of hearths, solitaries, and nine-sister circles that focus on research and teaching. The Sisterhood was founded by Jhenah Telyndru in 1995 as a reflection of her Avalonian study, which began in earnest in 1988. With a focus on research and teaching, the SOA was established to serve as a receptacle of lore and wisdom for all aspects of the study of Avalon, as well as to act as a medium for community-building for all who are beckoned to her shores. Over time, it has evolved to become a sisterhood in truth, united in a training of utmost discipline, and a dedication to reestablishing women's connections to a strong Celtic-based Western Tradition. Through study,

research, and personal workings, we are once again recall-
ing our heritage and fulfilling our sacred trust.

The Sisterhood of Avalon is an incorporated nonprofit
organization currently seeking 501(c)3 status. It is our
belief that, within this structure, we will be able to offer
increasingly effective and assessable methods of encour-
aging each sister to grow, heal, and become the reflection
of her personal Goddess Vision. In this spirit, the SOA
presents wise women's teachings which serve to midwife
the emergence of the priestess within.

Our approach to entering the Realms of Avalon is
through the application of techniques found in the Western Mystery School. To this end, we feel that a foundation
in Western Magick is essential. With these tools, we can
gain access to Avalon and her Mysteries.

We follow a Goddess-centered Path and work with
the Welsh pantheon. We feel that the female path is different from that of the male path; they are equal, yet opposite. Although we honor and acknowledge the male
aspect of Deity, we work only with female, passive energies, and work only with Goddess forms. We work strictly
within the confines of the Avalonian archetype. Although
we honor all goddesses as one, we work only with the faces
of the Goddess specific to Avalon. Of course, our sisters
may explore what they will of other Paths as well, but our
ritual workings are strictly keyed to Avalonian energies.

We do not pray to the Goddess to ask her to change
our lives. We do not utilize manipulative magicks of any
kind. We believe that we change the world by changing
ourselves. The Goddesses of Avalon work *with* us to effect
that change—to attain the goal of inner transformation—
for through issue resolution and soul healing, we become
closer to the Divine within ourselves.

We trust in the wisdom of the universe. We trust in
the universe's ability to maintain order and balance of its

own accord. We work to untangle the snares of personal soul-debt, while honoring its workings and recognizing our inability to see the full tapestry. It is thus, with humility, that we dare not meddle. It is not for us to change the Path of others—only they themselves can do so, and only thus are life lessons learned.

We strive to heal ourselves and gain inner clarity, so that we are not ruled by the unconscious motivations of our shadow sides. When we see with new eyes, we expand our perception of the universe and our place within it. We do not seek psychism for its own sake. "Psychic" abilities (that is, the Sight) are the by-product of our work, not the reason for it.

Although we acknowledge and honor the wisdom and accomplishments of our sisters with community-based recognition of their attainment, we believe that all true shifts of consciousness and initiations come *only* from the hand of the Lady herself. Through issue resolution, there is an increased ability to see with clarity and separate ourselves from issues of power and ego. Only when one can bypass ego and find joy in service rather than power, can one hear with clarity.

We work to understand and intimately know the powers of Land, Sea, and Sky, for through them we can understand the ways in which energy works both within and without. We seek the illumination of Awen through our workings and as part of our quest for wholeness and understanding both of Self and Goddess. We follow the lunar cycles for our holy day workings, not the Roman calendar, which was unknown to the ancient Celts. We work on the lunar crossquarters, the 13 full moons and the 13 dark moons.

We embrace, as our highest ideal, the concept of personal empowerment. There is no Book of Shadows to be memorized, no rote learning. We teach our students the tools they need so that they may come to their own wisdom.

Teaching someone the Elemental alignment of an herb only allows them to know the Elemental alignment of *that* herb. Teaching someone how to *determine* the Elemental alignment of an herb allows them to know the Elemental alignments of *all* herbs. We already have all the answers, we must only remember how to ask the questions.

We believe in the importance of understanding the culture from which the Avalonian Tradition emerged. Therefore, we encourage all areas of study within the Avalonian/ Celtic archetype. Immersion in this energy serves to open more doorways. Music, dance, song, chant, language, history, art, healing, ritual, divination, and so on, all have their Avalonian application, and are paths of service

Lastly, and perhaps most importantly, the Avalonian Path is experiential. It cannot be learned by reading books, or through observation of others. We must each actively seek our wisdom. This Path is also self-limiting and, therefore, requires the utmost discipline and dedication. A woman will only get out of the work what she puts into it. One cannot be an armchair priestess of Avalon. A woman who seeks to walk this Path must be willing to put it all on the line, have the courage to look her shadows square in the face, and be able to effect positive change in her life. The Path is endless; there is never nowhere else to go—there is only unwillingness to look harder. We are ever unfolding, ever seeking to conquer the mists which obstruct our sight.

Overall, the SOA is guided by the Morgen—the primary authoritative spokesperson for the thealogical direction of the Sisterhood of Avalon. She is roughly the equivalent of the Archdruid in other orders and Traditions. All women are equal in the SOA; simply, it is the service of the Morgan to keep strong and help manifest the vision of the Sisterhood. The Sisterhood also has level of attainment that reflect the amount of study a sister has successfully completed. These levels are: Aspirant, Novice,

Apprentice, Sister, and Wise Woman. To this end, the SOA sponsors the Avalonian Thealogical Seminary—a formal training program designed to teach individual sisters the wisdom of Avalon. We also have various administrative and fellowship bodies that handle the day-to-day affairs of the Sisterhood and assist with support and education of our members.

Above all else are committments to the Great Goddess, ourselves, our families, and our fellow Sisters of Avalon. In pursuit of these values, we believe the following statements are essential and timeless:

▶ We recognize and affirm the unique and intrinsic worth of each individual.

▶ We treat all those we serve with compassion and kindness.

▶ We act with absolute honesty, fairness, and integrity in our lives.

▶ We trust our inner intuitions and listen to the Goddess as she works her miracles through us.

▶ We strive to treat one another with loyalty, respect, and dignity.

▶ We are on a path of one with each other.

▶ We are as individuals true of heart and make a vow to harm none in our workings.

▶ We believe that, through our own behavior, we must take responsibility for our actions.

▶ As we walk with the Goddess on the Avalon Path, may she forever bless our work, as long as we hold to these ideals.

We work with the Mythic Cycle found in *The Mabinogion* and the writings of the Bard Taliesin. While we feel there are echoes of the Avalonian archetype found in Marion Zimmer Bradley's *The Mists of Avalon*, our tradition is not based upon what is depicted in that book. Rather, we hold that the book has served as a trigger for women around the world to seek the Mysteries of the Goddess, and to reawaken the quest for the Holy Isle.

We encourage our sisters to immerse themselves in some aspect of Celtic culture as an integral part of working in the Avalonian Tradition—language, art, music, folk-tradition, craft, literature, poetry, and so on—in order to better understand the context in which ancient Avalon existed. We stress fact over fantasy and discernment skills over imagination. We seek a balance between scholastic achievement and intuitive wisdom.

The Sisterhood provides a detailed resource list of Avalonian materials on our Website, where more information about our organization and tradition can also be found.

CONTACT

Website: *www.sisterhoodofavalon.org*
E-mail: BoardSecretary@sisterhoodofavalon.org
Address: The Sisterhood of Avalon
    PMB 139
    3330 Cobb Parkway, Suite 17
    Acworth, GA 30101

FURTHER READING

The Mabinogion
    A collection of traditional Welsh tales, there are various translations available.
The Mists of Avalon by Marion Zimmer Bradley
www.witchvox.com/trads/trad_avalon.html

ABOUT THE CONTRIBUTOR

Jhenah Telyndru is the founder and Morgen of the Sisterhood of Avalon (*www.sisterhoodofavalon.org*)—a fully incorporated nonprofit international Celtic Women's Mysteries organization that seeks to balance intuitive wisdom with scholastic achievement. She also serves as academic dean and lead instructor of the Avalonian Thealogical Seminary. She teaches Avalonian Intensive Workshops around the United States, facilitates pilgrimages to sacred sites in the British Isles, and is the author of the book *Awakening Avalon: Inner Sovereignty and Personal Transformation Through the Avalonian Mysteries* (2004). An initiate and priestess in the Avalonian Tradition, Jhenah has been dedicated to the work of Avalon for almost two decades. She holds a degree with honors in Archaeology, and her graduate study is in Chiropractic Medicine. Jhenah welcomes contact through her Website (*www.ynysafallon.com*).

BLUE STAR WICCA
By Cat Castells and Amy Douglass, Priestesses (Acknowledging the Writings of Devyn Christopher Gillette, Priest)

Blue Star Wicca is a Pagan Tradition founded in the mid-1970s. Originally established as a single coven in Pennsylvania, Blue Star evolved over the next two decades into a collection of more than a dozen covens all across the United States, all working in what is essentially the same framework and therefore recognizable as a tradition.

The ancestral coven of Blue Star was founded by a fellow named Frank Duffner, in 1975, and many of the folks who entered the Tradition in those early days are still practicing. It would be Frank's future wife and priestess, Tzipora Katz, and her second husband, Kenny Klein, who would have the most influence on spreading the Tradition to students across the country.

In the course of their career as traveling folk musicians, Kenny and Tzipora established small Blue Star study groups all over the country, teaching students during their brief visits once or twice during the year and later continuing to train via audiocassette, phone, and mail. These days, the number of trained Blue Star Initiates who live scattered across the country makes such long-distance learning largely unnecessary.

While Kenny and Tzipora subsequently left the Tradition, the Blue Star students and covens they left behind continue to dot the U.S. landscape, from coast to coast, though certain areas of the country may have higher populations than others. Examples of heavily populated Blue Star strongholds include Minneapolis, New Jersey, and the Boston metro area.

Blue Star practices mostly as a hierarchical, Mystery-based Tradition, with its roots in Alexandrian Craft. Most covens operate on a grove system, in which uninitiated members and students comprise an Outer Court, and Initiates make up an Inner Court. Traditionally, a coven (or circle) would include both inner and outer court members and would be presided over by a Third Degree High Priest and High Priestess. Obviously, while this may be the traditional ideal, the actual operation of Blue Star covens varies greatly from group to group. Smaller covens may have only one (or occasionally, no) Initiates, while large, extended covens may have three or more Third Degree Initiates.

There are three degrees of initiation in Blue Star, as is common to many Wicca Traditions. Prior to becoming an Initiate, Blue Star offers two other degrees, Dedicant and Neophyte. Dedicants may remain Dedicants forever, if they choose, while the degree of Neophyte is given specifically to prepare a student for initiation and is not meant to be an end point on anyone's Path.

You may have detected a theme so far in this description: no two Blue Star groups are exactly the same. We are almost as much a collection of rabid individualists as we are a Wiccan Tradition. We do, however, tend to share certain fundamental characteristics:

▶ A round altar stands in the center of the circle, with tools placed in specific locations.

▶ Liturgical songs are used for many actions of the circle.

▶ Children are welcome at most Blue Star circles.

▶ We celebrate the eight Wiccan Sabbats, as well as the 26 Esbats of the year.

▶ We acknowledge a number of Paths of Power corresponding to the Wheel of the Year.

▶ We tend to emphasize worship of the gods over the working of magick, and we often refer to ourselves as a "Teaching Tradition."

▶ We acknowledge and respect the entirety of the Wiccan Rede.

▶ We acknowledge and respect Tenets of Faith as cornerstones of our living philosophy.

▶ We acknowledge some gender specificity, in that our priests are male and our priestesses are female. We consider neither the Goddess nor the God to be preeminent, and likewise, we see neither men nor women as being superior. Rather, we seek to balance ourselves with regards to gender and deity.

▶ Most groups operate in a hierarchical structure.

▶ Each group is autonomous, though most of us seek to maintain a connection among various members of the Tradition.

There may be other interesting similarities or differences between Blue Star groups, but this list encompasses most of the fundamentals.

Blue Star asks its members to live their lives according to the precepts laid down in the Wiccan Rede and in the Tenets of Faith. We tend to respect the Law of Threefold Return and attempt to live our lives in a manner respectful of the gods, the earth, and other people. Many people believe a Blue Star education is significantly more strenuous than an education in some other Traditions, and Blue Star has historically admitted to demanding a fairly high level of dedication and commitment from its students.

Blue Star often defines itself as a "Teaching Tradition," and part of this teaching involves instructing students on their path to initiation and clergy status. According to Blue Star Tradition, priests and priestesses of Second Degree are considered clergy and may minister and teach to students, while Third Degree Initiates may receive ordination and may actually perform initiations themselves. Naturally, there are exceptions to this rule, and students at Neophyte level have occasionally run groves, while First and Second Degree Initiates have performed initiations. Blue Star is nothing if not pragmatic, and the elastic role of our clergy tends to demonstrate this characteristic rather well.

Most Blue Star groups observe the Esbats with a circle ritual, for which there is a common liturgical format. The exact execution of the circle may vary depending on the group, but most follow along a similar line. As stated before, Blue Star emphasizes worship heavily over the working of magick, though groups may perform magick in circle if they feel a need or desire to do so. Many Blue Star groups also teach the idea of living a magical life, and in so doing, encourage their members to worship the gods throughout the course of their everyday lives.

Blue Star has no formal written record of its tradition. Instead, most of the tradition is passed on orally from teacher to student. We do, however, have a deep appreciation for research and knowledge, and we encourage our students and Initiates to read a variety of materials encompassing areas as diverse as mythology and folklore, history and anthropology, divination and psychology. The best way to find out more about Blue Star is to seek out and talk to a Blue Star person in your area.

CONTACT

E-mail: acdouglass@eclipse.net (Amy Douglas)
    catpaw@bellatlantic.net (Cat Castells)

FURTHER READING

www.witchvox.com/trads/trad_bluestarwicca.html

ABOUT THE CONTRIBUTORS

Cat Castells is a Third Degree Initiate and priestess in Blue Star who runs an occasionally overwhelming teaching coven. Amy Douglass is a Third Degree Initiate and priestess in Blue Star. Both live on the East Coast, where they worship, teach, and live Blue Star.

BRITISH DRUID ORDER (BDO)
By Greywolf (aka Philip Shallcrass), Founder of the British Druid Order

Druidry is an indigenous, earth-ancestor spirituality rooted in the islands of Britain and Ireland. Historians generally associate Druids with the Iron Age Celtic culture that spread out from central Europe from about 800 to

200 BCE, yet the Celtic people of Gaul maintained that Druidry originated in Britain and that Druids from continental Europe came to the United Kingdom to study.

Our first written evidence of the word *Druid* comes from Roman texts of the turn of the millennium into the Common Era, when Roman armies were moving through northwest Europe and into Britain. The Druids were described as an intellectual and religious elite, working amongst the tribal peoples, holding power as custodians of their cultural and spiritual heritage, practicing their rites in urban shrines and woodland groves, revering the natural world as sacred and, in particular, honoring certain trees, plants, animals, rivers, lakes, and springs.

Druidry did not die out with the cultural changes introduced by the Romans, Saxons, or Vikings. It was an oral Tradition and survived as Druids continued to practice as bards, advisors, and priests, working with the power of the land and the wisdom of their ancestors, within a spiritual philosophy which naturally adapts, evolving through time. Clear remnants of the old teachings survived in the bardic colleges of Wales, Ireland, and Scotland that remained active until the 17th century, as well as in medieval manuscripts and folklore.

In modern practice, the Mother Grove of the British Druid Order (BDO) was formed in 1979. The Order is currently under the guidance of founders Philip Shallcrass (Greywolf) and Emma Restall Orr (Bobcat), as joint chiefs, their role being that of facilitators and guides. Philip is a Druid priest, musician, artist, poet, and writer. Emma is a priestess, a writer, Druid teacher, poet, singer, and soul counsellor. Both lecture and present workshops on many aspects of Druid Tradition. Both have practical experience in numerous magical, mystical, spiritual, and Shamanic Traditions, all of which they bring together in the BDO to create a unique brand of Pagan Druidry.

We draw inspiration from the sacred land and from our ancestry—the mud and blood of Britain, whose myths and mysteries are the well-spring of our Tradition. Druidry in its heyday is understood to have been a pan-European Tradition, and in our practice, we seek to recreate an understanding of Druidry as the native spirituality not only of Britain, but of Europe, Europeans, and European descendents living across the world. The process of restoration involves recovering a sense of the sacred in all areas of our lives so that we can begin to heal ourselves, our society and our land. Although we work with the long spiritual and cultural heritage of Druidry, we are not bound by any one aspect of it. We are not seeking to recreate a Druidry that may have existed 5,000; 2,000; 200; or 50 years ago. Seeing Druidry as a process of constant change and renewal, held within the natural cycles of regeneration and evolution, the Tradition is continually recreated to address the needs of each generation. The BDO works as an active agent in that process.

Our core beliefs honor the Ancestors and the gods of our people. They also emphasize spiritual energy known as Awen (flowing spirit). This allows for a dynamic, responsive structure that responds to the times, locations, and people involved, so that each discovers and walks a Path to joy, peace, healing, ecstasy, and the gods.

The Order seeks to pass on the Druid Tradition through hands-on teaching and direct personal experience. This is done via our network of groves and groups that gather to share teachings, ritual, and celebration, through camps, talks, workshops, sacred walks, sweat lodges, howling under the full moon nights, singing on high hilltop days, wading in the waters of life, forest gatherings, fire-dancing, spirit weaving, soul healing, eisteddfod (a Welsh festival of poetry and song), and recreation sessions. Through these events, we present and recreate the spirit of the Tradition.

The key aims of the Order are to be a source of inspiration and information for all those seeking to explore the native spirituality of these lands; to provide a network, bringing people together to share inspiration, celebration, learning, and ritual; to offer a real sense of community and belonging; and to be a forum for members and friends of the Order to express their creativity. For more information please consult the Website or write, enclosing an SASE, to the address provided in the following contact section.

> **A note from Trish:** *Greywolf went on to note something very important that should be remembered throughout this book. He says, "Let's be honest: no book is going to turn you into a Druid. That will take a lifetime or more of trials and tribulations, ecstasy, and experience." This is true of any Path. As a religion, whatever you choose will not be a "Shake 'n Bake," drive-through way to enlightenment. It will take time and serious effort to achieve your goals successfully.*

CONTACT

Website: *www.druidry.co.uk*
Address: The British Druid Order
   P.O. Box 635
   Halifax HX2 6WX, UK

FURTHER READING

American Druidism by Daniel Hansen
The Druid Source Book, edited by John Matthews
The Druids by Peter Berresford Ellis
Druidry by Emma Restall Orr
Druidry by Philip Shallcrass

Druidry: Re-Kindling the Sacred Fire, edited by Philip
    Shallcrass, British Druid Order
Elements of the Druid Tradition by Philip Carr-Gomm
The Pagan Religions of the Ancient British Isles: *Their
    Nature and Legacy* by Ronald Hutton
Principles of Druidry by Emma Restall Orr
Spirits of the Sacred Grove by Emma Restall Orr
    A Druid priest's personal journey through the
    sacred year.
Witches, Druids and King Arthur by Ronald Hutton
www.witchvox.com/trads/trad_bdo.html

ABOUT THE CONTRIBUTOR

Philip Shallcrass, aka Greywolf, is founder of the British
Druid Order. Philip is a musician, artist, poet, and author
of numerous books on Druidity. Emma is a writer, teacher,
and soul counselor. Both lecture and present workshops
on many aspects of Druid Tradition. Both have links with
other Druid groups in Britain and overseas.

CELTIC RECONSTRUCTIONIST PAGANISM (CR)
By Erynn Rowan Laurie, Aedh Rua O'Morrighu, John Machate, Kathryn Price Theatana, and Kym Lambert ní Dhoireann

Since the early 1980s, many individuals have been in
dialogue about what constitutes genuine, early Celtic religion and spirituality. The phrase "Celtic Reconstructionist"
(CR) began to gain common use during 1992, to describe
individuals who were trying to understand, research, and
recreate an authentically Celtic Path for modern Pagans.
Together and separately, we researched primary texts,

studied Celtic languages, did meditations and spirit journey work, wrote poetry and articles, and worked to gather
enough material to create the groundwork for a modern
Celtic Tradition—one that respects the ancient sources,
while rejecting those components of early Celtic religions
that are inappropriate for modern worshippers. We follow our inspiration, while remaining as true as we can to
the guidelines we find in early texts, the work of scholars
and archaeologists, and the practical aspects of what works
well for us. CR is a constantly growing and evolving path,
seeking learning, mystic and ecstatic experience, and the
intense life of the spirit.

Our Path is polytheistic and animistic. We believe there
are many deities, ancestors, and Nature Spirits who are
individual entities worthy of recognition, petition, and reverence. Most CRs believe that deities and spirits are active in the world and our personal lives, influencing us and
responding to prayer, offerings, and sacrifice. Deities and
spirits are seen as being similar to humanity in that they
have individual personalities, moods, and desires. They
are not necessarily all good and loving at all times, nor do
all deities get along with each other. All deities are respected, but not all are worshipped. CRs feel that, while
worship is appropriate, groveling before deity is not. Our
deities demand personal responsibility and that we act from
a position of strength and self-respect.

Some branches of CR have formal clergy; others do
not. CR is not a "religion of clergy" as Wicca and general
Druidism tend to be. Warriors, farmers, ranchers, writers, craftspeople, and many others may follow a household or homesteading Path, or worship and practice with
a group that has clergy. Craftspeople, writers, and others
may identify as *Aes Dána*, or "people of art." Individuals
may consult someone they consider clergy on their own
rather than being a part of a group. All are welcome,
whether they feel a pull toward service as clergy or not.

Commonalities of CR worship generally rest in philosophical agreement, rather than a consistency of ritual patterns between groups or individuals. CR practitioners do not cast circles; we believe the entire world is sacred, so we do not have to delineate our sacred spaces. As the four-Element model is incompatible with ancient Celtic cosmology, CR's experience the cosmos as three realms of Land, Sea, and Sky, along with an Otherworld or Otherworlds, which coexist with this one. The Otherworlds are considered real and accessible to those with appropriate skills. Fire, particularly fire arising from water, is central, and can be seen to symbolize *imbas* or *awen*—divine inspiration. Some see it as the central pivot upon which the cosmos turns—a spiritual equivalent to the world tree which grows through, and unites, the worlds. Most rituals involve offerings of food, drink, or other things to the deities, spirits, and ancestors; they are invited to our worship as our guests and the focus of our devotions. Divination methods are often used to see if offerings are accepted. Most CR practitioners also set up altars, hearths, or shrines in their homes, dedicated to these beings. Many altars don't take the standard Neo-Pagan form of tables with objects on them, but might be a place at the roots of a tree, a cairn of stones, or a small outdoor fountain or pond.

Many CRs consider each act of daily life a form of ritual. Some take inspiration from the *Carmina Gadelica* (a collection of Celtic folk prayers, charms, rituals, and omens) and create songs and prayers, to accompany daily tasks, or make offerings when harvesting. These rituals tend to be free-form and variable and are seen as being equally as or more important than major festival rituals or group rites. We don't believe that a ritual must be formal to be useful or effective, and such daily acts are in line with a tribal and culture-based way of life.

Magic, though not as central to CR as to some Pagan Paths, tends to be very pervasive in everyday ways. CR doesn't work in Platonic, Hermetic, or Ceremonial Magick formats, nor from those assumptions about the cosmos and spirit world. Ogam alphabet runes are a common vehicle for divination, as are dream and vision states, and omens interpreted from birds or cloud-watching. Poetry and music are frequently seen as a foundational component of CR magic. Charms modeled after those found in traditional Celtic folklore are often used, with poems sung over them to give them power. Reverence to deities and the help of spirits is almost always a part of CR magic.

We believe there are limits to what we can and should do, in an ethical and social sense, based on concepts taken from the Brehon Laws of Ireland and other traditional sources, such as the Instructions of Morann mac Main or the Welsh and Irish Triads. A common set of virtues followed by many emphasizes Truth, Honor, Justice, Loyalty, Courage, Community, Hospitality, Strength, and Gentleness.

Scholarship, mysticism, ecstatic experience, and personal inspiration are all necessary, though some individuals and groups will move toward one or another as primary for them. Research skills and wide reading are deeply respected, as is an understanding of history and a vocabulary of relevant terms in Celtic languages.

Men and women are equal in power and leadership within CR. CR has full and equal participation by sexual minorities—many of its founders and thinkers are gay, lesbian, bisexual, or transgendered. Feminism and Deep Ecology are seen by many as a vital component in their philosophy, practice, and personal work. Though many people of Celtic ancestry are drawn to CR, being of Celtic descent is not required. We give respect to all of our ancestors and teachers, whether or not they were Celts. CR is strongly anti-racist and welcomes people of all races, ethnicities, and colors who wish to follow Celtic deities in a CR style.

FURTHER READING

www.witchvox.com/trads/trad_cr.html

ABOUT THE CONTRIBUTORS

Erynn Rowan Laurie (*www.seanet.com/~inisglas*) is a *Fili* and one of the many founders of CR. She is the author of *A Circle of Stones: Journeys & Meditations for Modern Celts*.

Kathryn Price Theatana (*www.bandia.net*) is an EcoFeminist CR priestess, the founder of Nigheanan nan Cailleachan, Paganachd Bhandia, and a practitioner of Filidecht.

Aedh Rua O'Morrighu is a practitioner of Celtic spirituality since 1985 and a leader in several CR organizations.

Kym ni Dhoireann (*www.cyberpict.net/*) is a Scottish Reconstructionist on the warrior Path.

You can view the Website of John Machate at *www.thunderpaw.com/neocelt/*.

CENTRAL VALLEY WICCA (CVW): KINGSTONE TRADITION
By Kalisha Zahr

Note to the reader: To simplify things, when I refer to "Wicca," I am referring only to British Traditional Witchcraft, unless otherwise indicated.

Central Valley Wicca, or CVW, traces its origins back to adherents of the Old Religion who settled in the Central Valley of Northern California by the early 1960s. At that time, our ancestors did not refer to themselves as a "Tradition" of the Craft. They called themselves "Wicca." Tradition names came into use later.

According to our original custom, in the early days, a follower of the Old Ways was not told who their initiator's initiator was. Therefore, the identity of the person who first brought Wicca to the Central Valley of California remains a mystery; to this day, we only know of her by what is probably her Craft name. What *is* known is that she had ties to England and had most likely lived there—she was either British or had close connection to a British subject prior to settling in Northern California.

Today, the various branches (we used to call them *orders*) that descend from the Central Valley Wicca—and have developed into Traditions in their own right—include: Silver Crescent, Kingstone, Daoine Coire, Assembly of Wicca, and Majestic. Some of the offshoot Traditions from CVW have blended with influences from other related Pagan Paths, although most retain the core essence of CVW.

The rest of this essay is about the Kingstone Tradition. I leave it to those who are of the other branches of CVW to write about their Traditions, should they choose to do so. The Kingstone Tradition traces its origins directly to the Central Valley Wicca through both the Silver Crescent and Majestic lines. The Kingstone Tradition was formally established as an independent tradition in 1973, in conjunction with the formation of the New Wiccan Church. As an aside, the New Wiccan Church (NWC) is *not* a Tradition—it is an international association of individual members of various Traditions of Wicca. (Please refer to the contacts listed at the end of this article for more information about the NWC.)

In Kingstone, we acknowledge that all of creation stems from an unknowable Source, which is beyond human comprehension. Many of us view this Source as both immanent and transcendent. As Witches, we honour and worship the Old Gods of Nature—the Great Mother and her consort, the Horned God. We work primarily with the particular set of agricultural-pastoral-based deities of our ancestors in

CVW. Kingstone Initiates may also work with other additional deities as they see fit.

We seek to experience and understand the cycles and tides of birth-life-death in our daily lives through a personal relationship and a direct connection with our Gods, our ancestors, and the local spirits of the land. We believe in the power of magic, and use both traditional and experimental techniques to achieve our personal goals, as well as to help others in an ethical manner.

Initiation into a Kingstone coven means that, upon taking certain vows, one enters into an initiatory priesthood. The oaths taken state that the Initiate will protect and preserve the Craft, and the commitment to these vows is for life. In our view, initiation into Traditional Wicca is not the same as declaring oneself "Wiccan," as is so often seen today. To us, self-initiation is not possible, while self-dedication is of the utmost importance.

Kingstone Elders and their covens are autonomous. There is no central authority, yet those who teach understand that we hold a duty of care to pass the core tradition to our descendants as it was given to us. It is the role of the High Priestess and the High Priest to guide the coven with wisdom and love. We are dedicated to preserving and maintaining the rich heritage of our Tradition, and we also promote study and research in all related fields.

Kingstone groups are organized into covens. A coven consists of at least three people who are not all of the same gender. Kingstone covens may work either robed or skyclad (unclothed). To become Kingstone, one must be initiated in the traditional manner. Initiation is passed only from female to male or male to female. Same-gender initiations are not permitted in the CVW. We have a three-degree system. The normal minimum period between initiation and degree elevations is a year and a day, but this can vary.

The Kingstone Tradition is matrifocal but not matrilineal. Either a female or a male Third Degree Elder may operate a coven, but ideally, a cross-gender partnership is preferred. A Second Degree may Initiate (but only up to their degree) only under the authority and blessings of their Third Degree Elder. Although either a female or male may found a coven, it is preferable that a Third Degree female Elder cast the circle at initiations. This is in accord with traditional British custom.

The Kingstone tradition has a standardized Book of Shadows, whose copyright is held in trust by the New Wiccan Church. This standardized book is a compendium that is occasionally revised by the known Elders of the Kingstone Tradition, based on the continued research and review of the old CVW materials that are held in trust by the New Wiccan Church. Each Elder may also give out additional materials to their Initiates that they feel would be appropriate and beneficial to them. In keeping with traditional practice, Initiates are encouraged to develop their own personal book. Covens may have a group book, as well.

There is an obligation by each Elder of the Tradition to pass on their Book of Shadows as it was given to them. A genuine or authentic Book of Shadows cannot be purchased, nor can it be obtained in any other way, without the seeker having been properly initiated. Some may think that by picking up a Book of Shadows one could simply "set up shop," but in reality, learning the ritual form by rote only shows that one is able to do the mechanics. The Mysteries are a deep well that transforms the individual, and must be experienced directly.

In the Kingstone Tradition, some covens may share the cost for basic coven expenses by paying reasonable dues, or may simply "pass the Witches' hat" as expenses arise. Additionally, we have an obligation to maintain the privacy of other Initiates; therefore, to reveal the name or identity of another Witch, without their explicit permission, is not at any time appropriate. Overall, the Kingstone

Tradition closely follows the pattern of the original CVW, with only slight variations in form and practice. Specific details of our ways of worship, I cannot reveal here. Suffice it to say that our teachings focus on the development of a personal relationship with Deity, and a keen awareness and attunement with the cycles of Nature through ritual and in our daily lives.

CONTACT

Website: *www.newwiccanchurch.net*
E-mail: kalishazahr@yahoo.com
Address: NWC
    P.O. Box 162046
    Sacramento, CA 95819
    (For British Traditional groups only, and the New Wiccan Church, be sure to enclose sufficient first-class postage to ensure a reply.)

FURTHER READING

An ABC of Witchcraft by Doreen Valiente
Being a Pagan: Druids, Wiccans, and Witches Today by Ellen Evert Hopman and Lawrence Bond
    See the interview with Allyn Wolfe.
High Magic's Aid by Gerald Gardener
    Fiction.
The Meaning of Witch Craft by Gerald Gardener
Natural Magic by Doreen Valiente
Spells and How They Work by Janet and Stewart Farrar
Wicca: the Old Religion in the New Age by Vivianne Crowley
Wiccan Roots by Philip Heselton
    History.

The Witches' God by Janet and Stewart Farrar
The Witches' Goddess by Janet and Stewart Farrar
Witchcraft Today by Gerald Gardener
www.witchvox.com/trads/trad_kingstone.html
www.geocities.com/SoHo/tradlist.html
   Beaufort House Index of British Traditions.

ABOUT THE CONTRIBUTOR

   Kalisha Zahr was first initiated into the Craft in 1973. She is one of the founding Elders of the Kingstone Tradition and the New Wiccan Church (NWC), as well as a Gardnerian 3rd (Elder) and a Mohsian Initiate. As a crone-in-training, she has very little time these days for Witch wars and other such nonsense in her life. Kalisha lives in Northern California with her husband and cats, with plans to eventually live in Hawaii on the Big Island. She works in administration and is a professional Middle Eastern belly dance instructor and performer. Her interests include Mystery religions, mythology/folklore/Craft lore, divination, "core Shamanism" and related techniques, herbs, gardening, candle making, the healing arts, dance, and anything having to do with cats. She enjoys travel and is known to dabble in painting with watercolors or acrylics and writes the occasional article from time to time.

CHRISTIAN WITCHCRAFT
By Jesus Gypsy

A note from Trish: *Both this entry and "Esoteric Catholic/Cherokee" by Ambrose Hawk show us that Neo-Pagan Traditions can exist peacefully beside Christianity, when we apply a little creative vision to the mix. I know that some Neo-Pagans still have knee-jerk reactions to the church of their youth, but as you read, I think you'll see this is nothing like that.*

Our Path was founded in March of 2000, however we suspect many Christian Witches have practiced privately since the ministry of Jesus Christ began. Though no leader is required in our group, I have written all ceremonies and attached one such ceremony and spell with the approval and participation of the group. We have rather formal ritual times and informal ones as well. We take turns acting as ceremonial "priestess" during formal circle castings.

The group started because, as Christians, we were drawn to Witchcraft but would not give up Jesus to practice the Craft as traditionally taught. Christians could not accept the use of Witchcraft in their worship, and Witches could not accept Jesus as Lord in theirs. We needed fellowship and support of others who believed as did we. Most of us began as solitary practitioners and then found one another and created the small coven. We welcome visitors, but by invitation only.

As one might expect, we do not worship, pray to, or call on other deities. Only the Holy Father (the God of the Bible) and Jesus are worshipped or called upon. Spells can be traditional or created but must also include a prayer as an ingredient. Casting circles, divination, and all other forms of traditional magic are practiced, so long as worship, prayer, and power sought are focus on God the Father and Jesus. We believe and practice the Golden Rule, the Rule of Three, and the Wiccan Rede (in that order). When resolving conflict or establishing group doctrine, we will always err on the side of Christian practices, when in doubt.

ON BEING A CHRISTIAN WITCH:

You know what? I'm going to stop resisting being an oxymoron and start celebrating it. Am I an oxymoron? You bet your little booties I am. I am a doubting believer, a gentle warrior, a laughing mourner, a spiritual body, a "straight queer," a liberal conservative, an adult child, a weeping celebrant, an honored outcast, a human animal, a true fiction, a sincere hypocrite, an unconscious consciousness, a real fantasy, and a Christian Witch!

I am a nothing that is something, who hears sounds in silence, sees mystery in the common, embraces the sacred in the mundane, and finds wisdom in fools. I follow an oxymoron who said that the first are last, that the cursed are blessed, that dying is how one finds life, and that the greatest of all is the slave of all.

The oxymoron who called power weakness, riches poverty, and glory shameful, and who called weakness power, poverty riches, and shame glorious. The oxymoron who said all the Kingdom of Heaven is smaller than a mustard seed. The oxymoron who put "sinners" before "saints" and beggars before kings. The oxymoron whose crown was thorns, whose throne was a cross, and whose greatest victory was the greatest tragedy of all time; the One who wins by losing; the One who fills by emptying; the *God* who is *human*. The Oxymoron. The Paradox.

The Mystery. The Contradiction. The Dialectic. The Oxymoron.

Yes, call me an oxymoron, put me in the camp outside the city, with all the Sages, and all the Shamans, and all who have stood between worlds. I am a Christian. I am a Witch.

For formal circles, we prepare ourselves by not consuming alcohol or drugs beforehand and by cleansing ourselves in a ritual purification bath of herbs of our choice. We wear head coverings, linen tunics, a sash, bare feet, and tie back our hair. These are in accordance with how the Jewish High Priest was commanded by God to prepare for communion.

Our altar setup consists of a rectangular wooden table covered in gold cloth. The top row of implements represent God: (left) Bible, (center) white God candle and acacia wood cross, (right) olive oil lamp. The second row represents remembrance and offering: (left) bread and goblet of wine, (center) offering plate, (right) incense censor. The third row represents man drawing near: (left) bowl of salt, (center) bowl for mixing salt and water, (right) bowl of water. Finally, the bottom row represents man: (left) cauldron, (right) Torah pointer (instead of a wand) and athame.

Following is an example of a ritual for binding sinful habits (only the Lord can provide forgiveness, but this tangible ritual will reinforce it to your body, mind, and soul).

BINDING SINFUL HABITS

▶ Perform during waning phase of the moon (change, removal, obstacles, separation).

▶ Take a purification bath (any purification herbs you prefer, but include sandalwood oil or chips, as the Lord instructed it as part of the purification/protection ritual in Leviticus 4).

▶ Write the sin on paper and roll it like a scroll. Tie to a thorn cross with string, then anoint with sandalwood oil (if you cannot find a thorn cross, also called *Goddess needle*, use any suitable substitute, such as a cinnamon stick). Burn and recite:

> *My God, my King, my everything,*
> *I bind this sin with symbolic string.*
> *Forgive me Jesus, my iniquity;*
> *bid fire destroy and part from me*
> *And cast into the depths of the sea.*
> *Thank you, Lord, in praise I sing;*
> *Freedom's heart is rejoicing.*
> *The one true God, I praise thee;*
> *Heaven and Earth, eternally,*
> *join in praise to our King.*

CONTACT

E-mail: jesusgypsy@email.com

CHURCH OF ALL WORLDS (CAW)
By Iacchus

A note from Trish: *It is my understanding that, like many other organizations, the CAW has undergone some changes in leadership and focus in the last few years. However, this article provides a good, timeless overview of what the CAW was intended to be and do within our community.*

The Church of All Worlds (CAW) is one of the oldest incorporated Neo-Pagan churches in the United States. Among its members are people of various faiths, including the Abrahamic Traditions. CAW has an international membership that includes a board of directors, an ordained priesthood (of women and men), and a fellowship of consecrated members, called *scions*, who are dedicated to the service of the church. It has a process of personal development delineated by nine circles (stages) that can lead to the priesthood, local congregations called *nests*; and various subsidiary organizations. CAW promotes lifestyles that support personal freedom and responsibility, environmental stewardship, progressive and cooperative social order, and pluralistic democracy.

In 1962, CAW evolved from a group of friends and lovers who were, in part, inspired by the science fiction novel *Stranger in a Strange Land* by Robert Heinlein. These people created a religious organization that was recognized as a church by the federal government of the United States on June 18, 1970. They named this religious organization the Church of All Worlds, after the church founded by the protagonist Valentine Smith in the book.

The Church's organizing spiritual and social values include a belief in immanent Divinity, a pluralistic perspective towards religion, living in harmony with Nature, self-actualization, deep friendship, and positive sexuality. From the beginning, the Church's spiritual and social concepts and values were recognized as Pagan and then later as Neo-Pagan. As CAW continued to develop, it was influential in the growth of the broader Neo-Pagan movement and, in turn, was influenced by it.

CAW believes that the nature of our universe and planet is a manifestation of Divine being. As such, the nature of human being is an expression of Divine being.

In recognition of this, we greet and honor one another with the phrase "Thou art God" or "Thou art Goddess."

A fundamental sacrament and rite of CAW is a communion of souls called *Water-sharing*. In this rite, participants share water with one another. "Thou art God" or "Thou art Goddess" is similar to the Hindu greeting of "Namaste," which means "the Divine in me greets the Divine in you." "May you never thirst" is spoken when the shared water is drunk. Because water is essential to all known life on this planet, it is seen as being very precious. CAW envisions Water-sharing as a way of honoring this preciousness. This symbolic act also recognizes that one believes Divine Being is a living experience in all humanity. The phrase "never thirst" serves as a reminder of one's conscious connection with living as an experience of Divine Being.

CAW does not ask or require members to give up their religious affiliation or beliefs, as long as they share CAW's common values. One of these core values is a pluralistic attitude toward life and religion. It believes a pluralistic acceptance of a diversity of belief systems fosters religious freedom and peace within humanity. As a result, the religious/spiritual orientations of CAW members may include animistic, polytheistic, monotheistic, and monistic concepts.

CAW encourages its members to create and recreate rituals and myths that attune their life with Nature, bring honor to and communion with Divinity, reflect its values, and build community. One such myth is the vision that our planet is an individual living system, a Goddess, variously named Mother Earth or Gaia. Many members believe themselves to be children of this Goddess. This myth expresses the basic CAW tenets that our planet and life on it are sacred and that responsible stewardship of life and its environment is an act of worship.

CAW believes that humanity needs to be in harmony with its Self, for the Self is seen as a manifestation of divine immanence in Nature. It sees the human Self as the seed pattern and potential of the human soul. As such, the soul is a "system of becoming" that seeks to actualize its potential of the Self. Self-knowledge and actualization make it possible for the Self-conscious creation of harmony between humanity and Nature. This harmony is part of the human potential and is a primary religious goal and quest for CAW.

CAW encourages deepening or increasing intimacy in friendship. This it calls *growing closer*. Continued growing closer is characterized by increasing affection, affiliation, and intimacy. To foster this and the development of water-kin and tribe, CAW has religious communities called *nests*. The nest is the basic local organizational and congregational unit of CAW. A nest is a group of three or more members who come together to learn, discuss, and creatively practice the values and purposes of the church. Just as a nest in nature provides life with a means and context for growth, a CAW nest provides an individual member with a community and culture to foster self-actualization and communion with the Divine.

CAW encourages responsible reproductive strategies and choices. Men and women share the responsibility for pregnancy prevention and child rearing equally in CAW. Additionally, CAW believes that sexuality is an expression of the Divine. To honor this belief, CAW values and encourages *positive sexuality*. Positive sexuality is the affirmation of ethical sexual behavior and the pleasure-seeking instinct for the fostering of social bonding, including communion with one another and Divine being. Consent and peer-ship are the basis for ethical sexual behavior and positive sexuality. The expression of positive regard in human sexual behavior is essential for positive sexuality. CAW encourages nudity as a sacred practice for those who are called to do so within the privacy of a nest, in a secluded natural environment, or at "clothing optional" gatherings. Further, CAW believes if one chooses to be naked in one of its private rituals, it can be a sign that one is free.

CAW recognizes and blesses a variety of committed sacred sexual relationships as marriages. These marriages may or may not be sexually exclusive and may be monogamous, polygamous, or polyamorous. This variety of committed relationships not only reflects the ethical freedoms that CAW supports, but also reflects the historical and anthropological facts showing that humanity has practiced a wide variety of committed sexual relationships called *marriage*.

CAW is a religion, a system of values, customs, and ideas, organized in an organic fashion. It will grow, develop, and evolve in a way that brings about the best in humanity and honors Divinity.

CONTACT

Website: *www.caw.org*
E-mail: ingkj@mwt.net

FURTHER READING

www.witchvox.com/trads/trad_caw.html

ABOUT THE CONTRIBUTOR

Iacchus is a priest of CAW, licensed social worker, and certified sex therapist. You can visit his Web page at *www.caw/org/clergy/iacchus/index.html.*

CIRCLE CRAFT
By Selena Fox

A note from Trish: *I finally got to meet Selena last summer, after years of playing e-mail tag. Talk about energy plus! The beauty of her work is that she really focuses on people—there's no big-name-Pagan syndrome in her personality, just warmth and amazing determination.*

Circle Craft began in 1971, established by Selena Fox, but it also incorporates some aspects of older Paths. In the realm of Circle, each practitioner has had an influence and is part of the diversity that is this Path. Selena, the founder, has emphasized multiculturalism, ancestors work, and work with spirit of place in her teachings. Nils Holge brought his native Latvian Pagan influence in Circle Craft's early times; Dennis Carpenter, his humanistic psychology orientation in the 1980's.

The Circle Craft Tradition was initially known as Circle Wicca, during the 1970s, and then was called Wiccan Shamanism during the 1980s and 1990s. At the beginning of the 21st century, Selena Fox changed its name to Circle Craft, in order to distinguish it from the many other forms of Shamanistic Wicca and Paganism that had emerged in the United States and elsewhere.

Central to the Circle Craft Tradition is divine communion in and with Nature, plus the developing and sustaining of spiritual relationships with the Divine, both as a great interconnecting Unity, or Spirit, and with the Divine in multiple sacred forms, including deities, ancestors, Elementals, and Nature Spirits. Deities honored include both goddess and god forms. Circle Craft is animistic, and practitioners also develop sacred alignments with the spirits of particular plants, creatures, and places. The Circle Craft worldview is panentheistic, recognizing the sacred both as immanent, or indwelling, as well as transcendent.

Whenever possible, Circle Craft rituals are held outside in natural settings. Seven sacred forces, realms, and directions are invoked and honored in rituals: Earth in North, the physical realm; Air in East, the mental realm; Fire in South, the behavioral realm; Water in West, the emotional realm; Cosmos for "above," the universe; Planet for "below," the biosphere; Spirit in the center, the all encompassing spiritual realm and the interconnecting center that is Divine Unity. Ritual Circles are cast clockwise, beginning in the North, and usually the main altar is in or near the center of the Circle.

Circle Craft practice is enhanced by the use of ritual tools. These include, but are not limited to: altar and altar cloth; candles and matches; incense burner and incense; feathers; wand; staff; chalice of water; pentacle and/or dish of salt, soil, or herbs; quartz crystals; sacred art, such as images of deities; rattle, drum, bell, and other musical instruments; broom; cauldron; seasonal symbols; sacred foods and beverages; divination tools, such as tarot and runes; ceremonial garb and jewelry; and spiritual journal and pen. Blades may be used by individual practitioners, in personal work and in certain group rituals, but are not essential tools in this Tradition. The scourge and measure are not used. Most practitioners wear some form of consecrated jewelry, such as a pentacle, or an amulet known as a *Spirit bag*.

Dress in Circle Craft group rites is diverse, reflecting individual preferences and expressions, with some dressing in robes, some in ancestral folk costumes, and others in street clothes. Color of dress usually reflects one or more hues associated with the seasons. These include: black, orange, and indigo at Samhain; red, green, white, and gold for Yule; white and red at Imbolc; pastel green, yellow, and lavender at Spring Equinox; bright green, blue, and multi-colors at Beltane; green, gold, and yellow for Summer Solstice; green, gold, and brown at Lughnassad; and yellow, brown, orange, red, and purple for Fall Equinox. Both women and men, as part of spring and summer festivals, sometimes wear garland crowns fashioned from vegetation in season.

In the Circle Craft Tradition, the spiritual year begins at Samhain and includes the eight Sabbats, plus the celebration of Full and New Moons. Community celebrations of the eight Sabbats are multicultural. Bonfires and ecstatic drumming and dancing are usually part of seasonal celebrations.

Initiation by a teacher or group is not required in order to be a Circle Craft practitioner, but this is an option for those who complete a course of study and meet other requirements, including a preparatory outdoor vigil in a natural setting. Circle Craft principles include: Harm None, Be of Service, and Live in Balance. An important part of personal and group spiritual work is healing, and one or more modalities may be used to direct healing to others or to self, such as guided imagery, therapeutic touch, work with crystals and herbs, movement, drumming, and chanting. Work with dreams, meditation, and intuition are also important dimensions of Circle Craft study and practice. Additional information about the Circle Craft Tradition has been published in periodicals, books, and on the Internet, but much continues to be transmitted by word of mouth and guided experiences at study sessions and festivals. An online course is planned for the future and is currently being developed.

FURTHER READING

www.circlesanctuary.org/
www.circlesanctuary.org/circle/articles/circlecraft/
  circlecraftpath.html

ABOUT THE CONTRIBUTOR

Selena Fox is High Priestess of Circle Sanctuary and the founder of the Circle Craft Tradition. She guides Circle Craft rituals and learning experiences each month at Circle Sanctuary land in Wisconsin as part of Craftway Circle (*www.circlesanctuary.org/craftway*). She also appears regularly at other gatherings and festivals.

CORRELLIAN NATIVIST TRADITION
By Rev. Wendy Eversen, Hight Priestess

Originally the Correllian Tradition was not always known as that. The Tradition was founded by Orpheis Caroline High-Correll in 1879 (1479 Pisces). She was a woman of Scots-Cherokee ancestry and is claimed by some members of the High-Correll Family to have been a Scottish Traditional Witch. She was also a practicing psychic, a spiritual healer, and an herbalist. She spent many years traveling with her husband, John Correll.

In creating the Correllian Nativist Tradition of Wicca, Orpheis Caroline drew upon her Native American heritage, as well as the ideas of European Witchcraft, Spiritualism, and Hermetic views. The early history of the Correllian Tradition is a little unclear, with familial and religious structures wholly interconnected. But we do know that the family followed a very formal, matriarchal, and matrilineal structure, with its roots in Cherokee custom, from which the current office of the Correllian Tradition derive their form.

No two Correllian groups are exactly the same. We are almost as much a collection of individualists as we are a Wiccan Tradition. We do, however, tend to share certain fundamental characteristics:

> ▶ We all honor the ancestors from whence we came, and we living Correllians, when our turn

comes to cross over, will also remain active in the Tradition, for it is a commitment of more than one lifetime—a multi-generational project of transformation and regeneration of the Earth and its cultures—that will take many lifetimes.

▶ We celebrate the eight Wiccan Sabbats, as well as the 26 Esbats of the year.

▶ We tend to emphasize worship of Deity over the working of magic, and often refer to ourselves as a "Teaching Tradition."

▶ We acknowledge and respect the entirety of the Wiccan Rede—and we also believe that the Rede is not open for interpretation (from our perspective).

▶ We acknowledge and respect Tenets of Faith as cornerstones of our living philosophy.

▶ We seek to balance ourselves with regards to Nature and Deity.

The Correllian Nativist Tradition of Wicca asks its members to live their lives according to the precepts laid down in the Wiccan Rede. We tend to respect the law of Three and attempt to live our lives in a manner respectful of Deity, the Earth, and other people. Many people believe a Correllian education is significantly more strenuous than an education in some other Traditions, and the Correllian Nativist Tradition of Wicca has historically admitted to demanding a fairly high level of dedication and commitment from its students.

The Correllian System allows freedom to decide on your own Path. After completing the first degree, you can then decide if you wish to become a member of the clergy or just use what you have learned for your own personal knowledge and growth. If you decide to become a member of the Tradition, there are two Paths that you can take.

One is becoming an Outer Court Member, which is if you wish to enter the Correllian Tradition but not become an initiated clergy member. The other is becoming an Inner Court Member, which makes you an initiated clergy member of the Tradition.

Most Correllian groups observe the Esbats with a circle ritual, for which there is a common liturgical format. The exact execution of the circle may vary, depending on the group, but most follow along a similar line. As stated before, the Correllian Tradition emphasizes worship heavily, over the working of magic, though groups may perform magic in circle, if they feel a need or desire to do so. Many Correllian groups also teach the idea of living a magical life, and in so doing, encourage their members to worship Deity throughout the course of their everyday lives.

The Correllian Nativist Tradition of Wicca has a formal written record of its tradition, which can be obtained through any one of the Temples or Shrines listed at *www.correlliantradition.com/temples.htm*, through the Tradition itself (by way of Correspondence Courses provided by some Temples/Shrines), or by way of the online teaching facility known as Witchschool.com. We also have a deep appreciation for research and knowledge, and we encourage our students and Initiates to read a variety of materials encompassing areas as diverse as mythology and folklore, history and anthropology, divination and psychology. The best way to find out more about the Correllian Tradition is to seek out and talk to a member of the Correllian Tradition in your area.

CONTACT

E-mail: tapu@witchschool.com
    donlewisHP@aol.com (Correllian Nativist
    International)

oz@correlliantradition.com (Correllian Nativist Church Australasia)

FURTHER READING

www.correlliantradition.com
    Correllian Nativist International.
www.correlliantradition.com/oz
    Correllian Nativist Church Australasia.
www.witchvox.com/trads/trad_correllian.html

ABOUT THE CONTRIBUTOR

    Rev. Wendy Eversen, High Priestess, is Paramount Priestess for the Correllian Nativist Church Australasia Inc. and founding Temple Head of Whyalla's LaVeda Temple. Rev. Wendy studied with the South Australian School of Herbal Medicine and she has been practicing herbology ever since. With this background in mind, it's no surprise that Wendy is also well known as an author of "Herb Wisdom" in the Pagan Alliance's *Silver Wheel Magazine*, as well as a regular contributor to Pagan Awareness Network's (PAN's) *The Tapestry* magazine, and she has written countless courses especially for the Tradition and for Witchschool.com. She has even produced an "Herb Wisdom" CD.

COVENANT OF UNITARIAN UNIVERSALIST PAGANS (CUUPS)
By Splash and Andy

A note from Trish: *For many Neo-Pagans, the Unitarian Universal (UU) Church has been a god-send (or goddess-send!). It provides a well-established religious structure within which we*

can maintain our beliefs and practices. Being of
a mixed-faith family, my husband and I were mar-
ried by a UU minister, which is but one of the
advantages this philosophical system offers.

At 1985's Unitarian Universalist General Assembly (UU GA) in Atlanta, Georgia, CUUPS—the Covenant of UU Pagans—was envisioned by Dr. Christa Landon, Rev. Michael Boblett, Rev. Leslie Phillips, and Ms. Linda Pinti, and introduced at the Covenant of the Goddess Grand Council, a non-UU Wiccan authority. A year later, in Rochester, New York, the fledgling UU organization was announced to the UU GA, and in 1987, began presenting programs and adopted its statement of purpose and bylaws.

CUUPS secured independent affiliate status when the 1988 California GA ratified those bylaws. CUUPS' biannual Fall Convocation was kicked off in 1990, in California, and continues to provide a forum for addressing issues of concern, networking, and worshiping together. Major UU Pagan accomplishments include the incorporation of significant Earth-and-Goddess-centered material in the UU hymnal, as well as the adoption of a sixth source (part of the UU belief structure)—Earth-centered spiritual Traditions—as a formally recognized UU religious root. Today, CUUPS has grown to be 100 times its original size, has gained nonprofit status with the IRS, continues to facilitate networking among (and support for) UU Pagans nationwide, and helps to educated non-Pagans about UU Paganism.

UU Pagans generally believe that the sacred is an integral part of the web of life (and therefore, of us) and that no one spiritual Tradition holds exclusive rights to "The One True Way." Therefore, we embrace an eclectic, open-ended, and flexible Pagan Path.

CONTACT

Website: *www.cuups.org*

ABOUT THE CONTRIBUTORS

Splash has been practicing since 1996, and Andy, since 1997. They both have long felt closest to the sacred when connected with the natural world, and treasure the deeper connection that Paganism has nurtured within them. In particular, they like UU Paganism because it strongly encourages practitioners to explore and perhaps combine elements from various Paths, if it "works for them"; its leadership is democratic and open; and there are no rigid formats that one *must* follow.

CYBELINE
By Cathryn Paltine

As a reconstructional Tradition, our Path began some 9,000 years ago, with verified Traditions dating to 3,500 years ago. This ancient tie blossomed into something new, however. In 1995, after a lifetime of practice and research as a generic "Dianic" Pagan, the pieces started to fall into place, linking my research directly to the traditions of Cybele (known also as Magna Mater, Kubele, Kubaba, and several other variations). In 1999, Susan Davis and myself started public celebrations on the major solar holidays beginning with Meglamensia, whcih we now call the "Season of the Tree," at the Serpent Mound in south central Ohio.

Initially our practice centered on the "Gallae" of Cybele, with a primary focus on the practices used during the late Roman Republic, early Empire (circa 204 BCE–150 CE). The first public celebration was also a part of Susan's following the ancient Gallae Traditions, in preparation for her sexual reassignment surgery (she is a transsexual woman), which she had scheduled for March 24—*Sanquem* or "day of blood." In the fall of 1999, I ordained Marina Brown and Laura Potter as priestesses, joining Susan and myself.

The beginning of 2002, Marina Brown, Laura Potter, and myself purchased an old Catskill mountain inn, to be organized as a women's housing collective that became our *phrygianum*, which is a group home of Cybeline priestesses. In the summer of 2002, we were joined by Dr. Caillean McMahon. Today, our Melissea priestesses are Susan Davis, Marina Brown, Laura Potter, Caillean McMahon, and myself as, *Battakes*, or first among equals. Caillean, Susan, and myself have continued our research, which has literally exploded in the past year and half. We have around 40 people who attend our services off and on.

To understand us better, Cybeline practice was the source of the various "Mystery" religions of Greco-Roman period. We are dedicated to the worship of the Great Mother and, as were the Mystery religions, our practice is aimed at union with her while in our current lifetimes. Our beliefs are similar to Neo-Pagan in that we believe in reincarnation and maintaining a balance in the world. Seeing all as merely part of her, we really have no need for a rede or code, such as the Wiccan Rede, for if one truly understands that all around you is part of Mother—and your own part in that all—you will then treat other life, including the planet itself, with due respect.

As a Mystery religion, much of our teaching is in the form of stories and myths and reenactments of those stories. Our Tradition centers around the Great Mother as Cybele, Magna Mater. While Cybele was the source of almost all Mother Goddess Traditions, and her worship spanned 7,000 years in the ancient world, her name is barely known today because of the ruthless suppression of her worship, specifically by the early church.

Ritual garb varies with weather. Currently we are considering adopting the stola and palla of Rome as standard garb. Melissea and Gallae only rituals (female only) are clothing optional. Our temples are arranged at the junction of three paths with the main path having some sort of bridge to reflect entering a place between the worlds and a pine remembering Attis. Altar arrangement varies with the season and specifics, but always has a pinecone or two, symbolic of the rebirth of Attis, Cybeles son-daughter/consort.

Cybeline practice varies considerably from typical Pagan in that we do not call the quarters or cast a circle as part of ritual. The Earth is our circle and we believe, as Cybelines, that we already walk in both worlds. A typical celebration will have ecstatic dance, music, drumming, and the eating from the drum and drinking from the cymbal that was the origin of the Christian communion.

To find out more, visit the Website *www.gallae.com* or join us in an open celebration. We conduct open celebrations always on the solar holidays and welcome (by invitation) selected seekers to our full and new moon rituals. Women are always welcome, and men are welcome to the solar celebrations and by special arrangement for new and full moon.

RESOURCES

www.gallae.com

ABOUT THE CONTRIBUTOR

Cathy Paltine is cofounder of Cybeline and a reverend of the organization.

DIANIC TRADITION
By Jade River

The Dianic Tradition has been controversial since its beginning. Grounded in feminist principles, Dianics focus on female divinity, practice in women-only circles, and include large numbers of lesbians. This article explores Dianic Tradition and discusses it in the context of contemporary Neo-Paganism.

The Dianic Tradition grew out of the feminist movement. Many early feminists sought other avenues of spiritual expression, when they could not validate their activism within traditional religion. Women active in the women's movement began sharing their spiritual experiences in consciousness-raising groups. Women learned they shared similar spiritual feelings and had contradictory experiences within traditional religion. This prompted a search for a spirituality that supported a woman-centered perspective.

Into this void came Zsuzanna Budapest. Zsuzanna, called Z, recognized connections between Wicca and feminism. In 1976, her book *The Feminist Book of Lights and Shadows* formed the basis of Dianic Tradition. Now revised, expanded, and published under the title *The Holy Book of Women's Mysteries*, Z's book became and continues to represent the foundational principles of Dianic Wicca. This book and Z's charismatic presentation of its ideas ignited a movement.

A controversial element of early Dianic Wicca was the number of lesbians involved. In the early Dianic movement, lesbians formed such a substantial majority of those who identified as Dianic that, if one said she was Dianic, she was essentially "coming out" as a lesbian. In the 1970s, lesbian culture had not attained the acceptance it holds today and many mainstream Pagans responded to the presence of lesbians at Pagan events with distain.

From the mid-1970s until the mid-1980s, most Dianics were isolated within the women's community and largely unaware there was a broader Pagan community. The first encounters between "mainstream" Pagans and Dianics were controversial. When Dianics began attending Pagan gatherings they wanted to celebrate in women-only circles. Some mainstream Pagans found this upsetting. Because of the fervent belief in duality held by some mainstream Pagans, it was thought single-sex rituals would permanently damage anyone who participated. During one of the first women's circles at a mainstream Pagan gathering, husbands actually removed their wives from the circle to protect them from this perceived injury. Despite early difficulties mainstream Pagans and Dianics now interact with relative ease. Mainstream Pagans have come to respect the creativity of Dianics, while Dianics have learned to value mainstream Pagan traditions.

Across North America and, to a lesser degree, in other areas, Dianic Wicca became a feminist religion. Because of the isolation of women who practiced Dianic Craft, it developed as a very individualistic Tradition. There are, however, core beliefs among virtually all who practice Dianic Craft. They are:

▶ Belief in female divinity, most often referred to as "The Goddess."

▶ Celebration of Celtic holy days.

▶ An underpinning of feminist ideology.

▶ A belief that women's bodies are sacred.

▶ An honoring of women's experience as authentic.

▶ An understanding that patriarchal society does not reflect women's experience.

▶ No recognition of male Gods in ritual.

▶ A belief that only women-born-women truly understand women's experience.

Feminist Dianic Wicca focuses solely on the Goddess and is exclusively practiced by women. It does not espouse a dualistic female/male concept of divinity, believing instead the Goddess is the Creatrix and sustainer of the universe. Most Dianics, however, do not exclude men from their cosmology. They acknowledge all people, including men, as women's children and, therefore, a part of the Goddess's creation.

One might suspect that the Goddess celebrated by Dianics is Diana, however, this deduction is incorrect. Stemming from the multicultural roots of feminism, Dianics are global in their approach to divinity, believing the presence of the Goddess in all cultures unites all women.

Some Dianics believe in "spiritual virginity" and choose only to work with women. However, for some Dianics, being in a woman-only group is not the only way they celebrate their spirituality. These women find value in both women-only space and in mixed-gender groups. Unlike traditional religions, which espouse that one can only have a single religion and it must be your only religion, many women value multiple Pagan spiritual Traditions, Dianic being one of them.

Over the years, Dianic Wicca has changed and is no longer practiced solely by lesbians. In Dianic circles, one can now find women of all sexual orientations. Some circles consist entirely of lesbians, some of only heterosexuals, while others include women of all sexual orientations. Dianic circles are not open to transgendered individuals. Dianics believe a primary source of women's power is women's shared experience and women's biology. Although supportive of transgendered rights, Dianics believe this is not a Tradition that encompasses the experience of transgendered people. Otherwise, the basic beliefs of Dianics are those commonly shared by most Wiccans.

In terms of organizations, the oldest and largest women's religion is the Re-formed Congregation of the Goddess-International (RCG-I). Founded in 1984, RCG-I was the first officially recognized women's religion in the United States with affiliated circles and solitary members around the world. Congregation members embrace a variety of spiritual Paths, the common element among them being a belief in female divinity and a commitment to positive spiritual practice. RCG-I is a multi-traditional women's religion, however, a majority of the women in the congregation consider themselves to be Dianic. Information about RCG-I is available on the Web at *www.rcgi.org*.

The role of clergy in Dianic Wicca is quite diverse. Leadership in Dianic tradition can range from a nonhierarchical structure to groups with an acknowledged priestess. Several programs train Dianic priestesses. The oldest and largest of these is the Women's Thealogical Institute (WTI). WTI has trained numerous priestesses, a majority of whom are Dianic. WTI has numerous programs, including training for guardians and crones and training in Women's Mysteries called *Cella*. Upon completion, WTI participants can apply to be ordained. RCG-I ordains its priestesses each year in May, at its annual Priestess Gathering.

Dianic Wicca is a growing Tradition. The number of women in RCG-I has grown exponentially since it's beginning in 1984. There are now more than 2000 members of the congregation, half of which have joined in the last five years. With the vitality of a living Tradition, Dianic Wicca will continue to attract women interested in creating women's magic and honoring the Goddess.

FURTHER READING

Holy Book of Women's Mysteries by Zuzanna Budapest

Moonrise: Welcome to Dianic Wicca by Amber K
>   A pamphlet that describes Dianic Wicca in more
>   detail and is available from RCG-I (*www.rcgi.org*).

To Know: A Guide to Women's Magic and Spirituality by
>   Jade River

When God was a Woman by Merlin Stone

en.wikipedia.org/wiki/Dianic_Wicca
>   Wikipedia, the free encyclopedia.

www.rcgi.org
>   Re-formed Congregation of the Goddess, Inc.

www.rcgi.org/wti/wti.asp
>   Women's Thealogical Institute.

www.witchvox.com/lx/lx_dianic.html
>   Dianic Websites.

www.witchvox.com/trads/trad_dianic.html
>   Dianic Tradition.

ABOUT THE CONTRIBUTOR

Jade is the creator of the Women's Thealogical Institute, which was the first institute to offer an in-depth training program for women wishing to deepen their connection to spirituality or learn priestessing skills. She is the author of *Delphi: A Goddess Oracle* (Triple Crescent Press, 2002), *Tying the Knot: A Gender Neutral Guide to Weddings for Pagans and Goddess Worshipers* (Triple Crescent Press, 2002), and *To Know: A Guide to Women's Magic and Spirituality* (Delphi Press, 1991). Jade is also cofounder of the Re-formed Congregation of the Goddess—the first legally incorporated tax-exempt religion serving the women's spiritual community—and a vocal recording artist with Triple Crescent, a Goddess-oriented musical group.

DISCORDIANISM-ERISIANISM
By St. Hugh, KSC, KNS

Anyone familiar with the Discordians knows the difficulties inherent in describing a vibrant aspect of Paganism that claims to "have no definition." With one of the major trends of Discordianism being one of decentralization and disagreement, is there a way to adequately describe it? To be true to Discordia (the Latin name of our primary Goddess, Eris), I would have to say "yes, no, and maybe." Even though many people look at the plethora of our humorous writings and dismiss it as a religion, Discordians take their humorous traditions very seriously...to a point.

The foundation of the Discordian movement in modern times comes from the paradoxical writing collection known as the "Principia Discordia, or How I found the Goddess and what I did with Her when I found Her." It tells the story of two young men in a bowling alley who receive the first Erisian Revelation back in 1957 or 58. (In true Discordian fashion, which year is never cleared up.) The men go on a search of mythologies and discover Eris, the Goddess of Confusion, Chaos, and Discord. (Eris is also the Greek word for "strife.") They surmised that chaos underlies everything, including order and the followers of order: "Look around and you can see all of the chaos in everything just as much as you can see order." The two men declare themselves to be High Priests of their own madness and start a Discordian Society "for whatever that may turn out to be."

Today there are several active Discordian groups, known as *cabals*, that continue to develop and practice Discordian ideas and rituals. The organization of the groups within the Discordian Society (or without, as some groups will no doubt claim) is decentralized. Usually people will either join a preexisting cabal or, if Eris decides to give new revelations, will start their own cabal. Within cabals, there is usually an *episkopos*, who is responsible for the rituals, revelations, and organization. Thus it can be said that each cabal may choose its own organization. The major trend is towards non-hierarchy as episkoposes are known to hand off the leadership mantle whenever they see fit.

One of the main tenets of Discordianism is that "it is a firm belief that it is a mistake to hold firm beliefs." That said, it is possible (though highly disagreeable) to pin down a few ideas that are common among Discordians. One is a dedication to personal "illumination" by exploring as many belief systems as possible so that a person will realize the absurdity of taking any idea too far. Another idea is "if it makes you cry, it is real; if it makes you laugh, then it is probably true."

Discordians worship Eris, who is probably the most paradoxical being people could ever worship. If they don't worship her, then they explore her in some way or another. They see in her as a symbol of freedom from all constraints and a license to become the best person one can be. One thing we have in common with the very beautiful Wiccan Charge of the Goddess is the most famous Charge of Eris, which follows.

CHARGE OF ERIS

"I have come to tell you that you are free. Many ages ago, my consciousness left humanity, that they might develop themselves. I return to find this development approaching completion, but hindered by fear and by misunderstanding. You have built for yourselves psychic suits of armor, and clad in them, your vision is restricted, your movements are clumsy and painful, your skin is bruised, and your spirit is

> broiled in the sun. I am chaos. I am the substance from which your artists and scientists build rhythms. I am the spirit with which your children and clowns laugh in happy anarchy. I am chaos. I am alive, and I tell you that you are free."

To Eris worshippers, this is as evocative to us as the Charge of the Goddess is to Wiccans. With a charge so powerful, one can probably glimpse why anyone would become a Discordian.

In terms of conduct, Discordians adhere to the Chaoist idea that "nothing is true and everything is permissible." It sounds like a blanket endorsement for any sort of behavior. Even so, it is said that some religions preach love, compassion, law, and forgiveness, but result in hatred, disorder, and destruction. Discordianism preaches chaos, confusion, and disorder, and results in love, creativity, freedom, and laughter. The reason why an ethic of "everything is permissible" works within Discordianism is the ultimate respect given to the individual to work out their own approach to Eris. We do not believe in manipulating people or even trying to control their expressions, even if they disagree with us. And this idea comes from the idea that we are all free right now. If this sounds like anarchy, you may be right...maybe.

Many Discordians are also practitioners of other Traditions, such as Wicca or variations of Witchcraft. Eris worshippers, such as me, also have other deities. Some are even members of other religions, such as Buddhism— Zen is a particular favorite, and sometimes Discordianism is described as a "laugh happy Pagan Zen."

Granted, this description is a brief one and in no way could hope to capture the full spectrum of Discordianism. It is hoped that those who would like further information about the vast realm of Discordian esoterica and eristica will consult either some of the sites from the following list or their own pineal glands. If you think that Discordianism is just a bunch of silly craziness that makes no sense, then you probably need to look again. If you think that Discordianism is terribly confusing, we may have more in common than you think. If you think that Discordianism is something-or-other but can't quite grasp it, hail Eris, you may understand.

CONTACT

E-mail: aodh99@hotmail.com

FURTHER READING

Liber Kaos by Peter J. Carroll

Liber Null & Psychonaut by Peter J. Carroll

The Principia Discordia by Gregory Hill and Kerry Thornley

http://www.poee.org/
   The POEE Website.

www.23ae.com/files/apocrypha2.pdf
   The Apocrypha Discordia (available online only).

www.discordian.com/
   The Church of No Dead Saints Website.

www.geocities.com/tribhis
   The Purple Monkey Website.

www.geocities.com/tribhis/pathofchaos.html
   The Path of Chaos I (available online only).

www.geocities.com/tribhis/pathofchaostwo1.html
   The Path of Chaos II (available online only).

www.principiadiscordia.com/
   Online PD with forums.

www.verthaine.chaosmagic.com/
The Church and Book of Eris.
www.witchvox.com/trads/trad_discord.html

ABOUT THE CONTRIBUTOR

St. Hugh, KSC, KNS (triskell aka Tequilarius Malignatus) is a Discordian Pope (and so are you), who also happens to be an Episkopos of the Purple Monkey Mafia/Cabal in Chicago, Illinois—not that he claims any responsibility for their actions, however. Seriously, his real name is Hugh Scharland and, besides being a Discordian for several years, has been practicing Pagan Witchcraft since 1995 or 1996. He has studied Chaos Magic and also Vajrayana Buddhism. He is a poet and a photographer and is therefore chronically unemployed. He also enjoys watching sunrises. Kallisti!

ECLECTIC WICCA AND PAGANISM

This is going to be difficult. The eclectic is perhaps the most cat-like individual in terms of independent thought and creative adaptation. In the more than 100 surveys I received, the vast majority listed themselves as eclectic (or an eclectic blend). I believe this is a fair representation of our community on a larger scale too. Many have taken a mixed-Path approach, often due in part to being solitary practitioners. Following are just a few descriptions people gave for their Path.

ECLECTIC (BY DEBBY, RWOLF927@AOL.COM)

I've been practicing this Path for 20 years. I was born and raised in the fried-chicken-eating, foot-washing, joy-jumping, no-dancing, no-drinking, wear-your-best-on-Sunday, all-towns-are-controlled-by-the-Baptist-Church, do-you-know-Jesus, are-you-saved South. Due to a variety of factors, I remained an atheist until I was 24, quite happily, until I "got it."

When the wall between myself and Deity fell, I flirted with Catholicism, hung out with Baptists (Hmmm), and played around with Jewish folks. I rubbed Buddha's Belly, danced with the Hari Krishnas, and then I found (the hard way) that religion and spirituality have little or nothing to do with each other, so I found the books and I read it all. This lead me to believe that the small, still voice inside me is the voice of God, and that each and every one of us is a cell, a corpuscle, in the body of the Divine. (Some cells are helper cells, some are muscle cells, and there are some cancer cells, too.) I believe the Divine is so fantastically multifaceted that my little self is too small to see its wholeness.

ECLECTIC WICCAN WITH NATIVE AMERICAN, CELTIC, EASTER, PAN EUROPEAN, AND VOODOO (BY SHADOWSONG)

Voodoo traces back to African beliefs that were carried to Haiti and eventually brought to New Orleans via the slave trade. My mix is not altogether that new, but there is no definite founder. Ray Marlborough was a big influence on the acceptance of Voodoo folk magick in modern Paganism (I suggest reading *Charms, Spells, and Formulas* by him). I use lots of blanket archetypal images. But when I incorporate Voodoo into Wicca, I use a basic pantheon of spirits/deities referred too as the *Orisha* or *Loas*. Many of the deities are similar to those used in typical pantheons, so I find that it is easy to mesh the magickal systems.

SAMPLE LOVE RITUAL

This ritual incorporates my blend of Paganism with Voodoo:

Prepare an altar. Lay a red cloth upon it, for it is pleasing to the spirits. Lay representations of the Elements or anything else that is traditional upon the altar. In the center, gather a piece of red flannel, rose petals, a piece of rose quartz, cinnamon, star anise, rosemary, and basil. Also gather a lock of your hair and a piece of parchment with a ve-ve (a special Voodoo sigil) drawn on it to represent Erzulie, Orisha that rules love, or use another love symbol in its stead. Light a pink, a red, and a white candle in a triangle around the materials gathered for the spell. Place all of the ingredients within the red flannel and tie it up with cord or ribbon. Consecrate it using the four Elements, and return it to the center of the altar. Invoke the Goddess Erzulie through prayer or incantation and ask her to bless the gris-gris you have just made. Place your hands over it, to empower it and channel the power of Erzulie into it. Imagine the qualities of the lover you seek. Pour your desire for love into the gris-gris, and open your heart to the Divine. Seal the gris-gris by passing it through the candle flame and anointing it with a sacred oil, preferable rose, jasmine or lavender. Bind the candles together, and extinguish them in reverse order. Save them to re-empower the gris-gris, or bury them at a crossroads. Thank Erzulie for her aid. Clean the ritual area and remember to anoint the gris-gris once a week, on the same day you made it, to keep its powers strong as you carry it to attract love.

BLENDED ECLECTIC SOLITARY WICCAN (BY WIC, PRETTY-WICCAN@EXCITE.COM)

Basically, I follow the Wiccan Rede. I believe in the Divine, but I do not view it as an outside force. It is within each of us—plant, animal, human, earth, and sky. As an aid to focus, I will visualize the male and female aspects and, when speaking to others of like mind, use the words *lord* and *lady*. I follow the Pagan/Celtic calendar of Sabbats, Esbats, seasons, and so on, as it seems to suit me personally. I make use of intuition, empathic abilities, meditation, ritual, and magick. I also include alternative healing modalities, as I believe they are fundamental in my spirituality, which include reiki, stones, reflexology, and aromatherapy.

Ethically, I feel it's important to protect and honor nature and her beings; care for those less fortunate; be true to my word always; use my healing abilities for all, regardless of their nature; impact Mother Earth as benignly as possible; live a life of honor; and most important, know myself—the light and shadow equally well—and live in balance. I am vegetarian and a minimal user of animal products. I believe I should speak little and learn much.

For tools, I have a rather typical Wiccan alter set up in the southern corner of the upper floor of my dwelling. A blue heron feather, gifted to me by a native Shaman, is the only nontypical item. He had had a vision of me as a blue heron woman healing a community of mixed peoples, and its place on the alter reminds me that all of our belief systems are but branches of the same tree of life.

ECLECTIC NEO-PAGAN: EGYPTIAN, GREEK, SUMERIAN, NATIVE AMERICAN, AND HINDU FOCUS (BY JESSICA)

I believe in reincarnation—specifically that, when we die, we go to a lower realm where we work out problems that we had in our life, then we go to "summerland," where we either reincarnate or move on to higher realms closer to the universal spirit (God/Goddess in all his/her forms). I believe that all of nature should be revered as part of divinity, and that all plants, animals, and inanimate objects have their purpose in the world, whether they are meant for human use or some other purpose. In terms of Deity, all forms of gods and goddesses are just branches of the same divine power, but it makes it easier to tap into divine power if you apply a name and face to a particular aspect. Here's a sample meditation for finding your animal guides/totem.

FINDING AN ANIMAL GUIDE/TOTEM

Have a candle burning and some incense (whatever helps you get into a meditative state). You may also place figures of different animals around you, and maybe play a CD of nature sounds—whatever you feel will help. Sit in whatever position you normally do for meditation. Picture yourself standing at the edge of a high cliff. You get the urge to jump, and as you do, you begin to fly over an ocean. You see an island after a bit—an uncharted island. It is the island of animals. You land on a beach; you hear animals all around you. Ask your spirit guide to appear to you. After a few minutes, your spirit guide should appear. Note: the average person has about nine spirit guides, but do *not* try to find them all in one meditation. It's okay if several animals appear to you in the first one, of course, but it wouldn't work out too well if you had a lion and a gazelle as spirit guides, now would it?

As you can see, the eclectic approach is truly a mixed salad of Traditions, blended with the dressing of personal vision. There is no one who can tell you exactly how to assemble an eclectic approach; you must, in the end, be your own guru and guide.

FURTHER READING

Baghavad Gita: As It Is by Swami Prabhupada
Gothic Grimoire by Konstantinos
Grimoire for the Green Witch by Anna Moura
Nocturnal Witchcraft by Konstantinos
www.geocities.com/ariadnemoondust/ancientpath.html

ESOTERIC CATHOLIC/CHEROKEE
By Ambrose Hawk

A note from Trish: *For another look at ways in which Christianity and Neo-Paganism mix, see the entry for Christian Witchcraft earlier in this book.*

There is a good chance that Brendan the Navigator established a missionary program about 600 AD, which influenced the Cherokee Religion. Such features as the sacred and secret name of God (the public version, "Yawoo," is suspiciously like "Yahweh"), a trinity (three elder fires look a lot like Father, Son, and Holy Ghost), and the four winds that look like the four evangelical cherubs from Ezekiel) are just the tip of the iceberg. Still, this is pure speculation.

What is true is that the Cherokee found Christianity to be "fitting" to what they would expect of the Great Spirit and became "Christian" en masse, while preserving their native ways and practices alongside their new faith. An interesting point, it was Catholic Esotericism that created the modern tarot and its interpretive methods. My father came out of this background and taught me. His own esoteric background was extremely eclectic...including not just his Cherokee/Christian childhood, but also Judaism and Buddhist monasticism. As for magical Christianity, per se, there are texts and amulets from Syria and Egypt that go back to the second century, at least!

In practice, I combine the "Great Commandments" (Love God, Love thy neighbor as Jesus loves her) with the Cherokee way of right relationships. No undue harm, no undue blessing, and quiet respect, even when ruthlessly hunting down an enemy. Hunting parties would not kill an animal that had not been included in their prehunt prayers, for instance. Following is an example of a solstic spell for consecration, derived from a Syrian Christian source, that I use to charge a jar of honey with healing virtue.

Solstice Spell for Consecration

AVE, DOMINUS! AVE, SOL INVICTUS!
Hail, Sun of rightousness, who shines upon
all the land. Come upon this (honey);
send your sacred fire into it; contain it
and reveal it in your holy light.

Manifest your rule above the 12 powers,
That this (honey) become the pane where
your generosity shines upon our desires.
In the name of your great archangel, Abraxas,
whose hand is stretched out over the primal rays
of the Cosmos, you must enlighten my heart.
Shine upon me that I may share your joy,
that I may perceive your wisdom.

Thank you, YHWH: holy, powerful One;
holy, immortal One; holy, wise, and all-knowing
One. Hail, bright and shining star.

for the joyful light you have shone upon me.
Kairos, Kyrios! Light of gladness,
light of the eons, light of joy, light of my eyes,
lamp of my body, YHWH Sabaoth.
Give me the sun as a garment and the moon for
a cloak. Carry me in the ship of the sun, that I
may sail through and over the tempest of evil.
Assign to me the rulers of the great planets,
their spirit, their intelligence, their mighty
powers, that I may share in the life of the stars
And be made worthy to behold your face.
As you love me, you must give me your glory
of the sun, you of the great number,
that I be guarded from all evil.

CONTACT

E-mail: ahawk@centurytel.net

FURTHER READING

Collections of works by James Moody
>   Good resources for non-tribal members. Moody was
>   a major ethnologist for the Smithsonian Institute
>   who published a lot of works to preserve the lore of
>   many Native American tribes and was considered
>   accurate by their own medicine men who referred to
>   his work as a reliable source. His Cherokee collec-
>   tion is about half in print; you should contact the
>   Library of Congress or the Smithsonian for access to
>   all of his work.

Medicine of the Cherokee: The Way of Right Relationship
by J.T. Garrett and Michael T. Garrett
>   Also contains a lot of information.

Meditations on the Tarot (anonymous)
   An extremely informative work.

ABOUT THE CONTRIBUTOR

Ambrose Hawk first emerged as an occultist due to the reckless experiments attempted by his friends during the occult fad of the 1960s. Ironically, this eventually led him into a deeper involvement with his church. Hawk spent six years as a seminarian, two of them in a Benedictine college and two of them at the Pontifical Institute at Catholic University of America in Washington, D.C. During this time, his Benedictine spiritual advisor chided Ambrose for not attempting to integrate the spirituality of his traditions into the more formal traditions of the Church. Since that time, Ambrose Hawk has sought actively to uncover the deepest links among the religious symbols and archetypes that all peoples share to some degree. Ambrose Hawk is the author of *Exploring Scrying*, from New Page Books.

FAERIE FAITH
By Cliff Landis

A note from Trish: *There are numerous Traditions calling themselves Faerie, Fairy, Fey, Feri, and so on. While some may be related in their foundational material, the practices—and some beliefs—vary greatly. Please keep this diversity in mind if you choose to explore this Path further.*

The Faerie Faith is a complex Pagan Tradition, with its own mystical system, the Beth-Luis-Nion Celtic Lunar Tree Calendar. The Beth-Luis-Nion system (named for the ancient Celtic Ogham alphabet) is a beneficial system that leads to an understanding of Nature, and a personal transformation of the student. Ours is a Dianic Tradition, and as such, places emphasis on the feminine in humanity, in Nature, and in God. For ease of reading, all pronouns will be in the feminine, according to that Tradition. However, it should be noted that individuals of both genders can and do enter the training of the Faerie Faith.

The Faerie Faith is a Tradition that has branched off from the McFarland Dianic Tradition (1970s). Through Mr. Mark Roberts and the High Priestess known as Epona, the Faerie Faith has been handed down over the years (since the 1980s). The name was most likely taken from *The Fairy-Faith in Celtic Countries* by W.Y. Evans Wentz, published in 1911. This book describes a variety of folk beliefs and practices in the past.

As a Shamanic and Mystery Tradition, the Faerie Faith has a training system and an internal hierarchy. The training of students of the Faerie Faith is a very complex and difficult process. As such, it tends to take a very long time (four to eight years, typically).

The rituals of the Faerie Faith can be split up into two categories: lunar rituals and passage rituals. Rituals are done outdoors, as long as weather permits. They are typically held in rural areas, using small stone circles laid out upon the ground. The sites for these circles are usually selected as those with the most natural energy occurring. To give you a feel for our rituals, during lunar rites, we share a Water ceremony in which everyone drinks from a common cup, as the priestess says:

> *"Share of my water and know that as the rain, it is the bringer of life. Share of my water and know that as the oceans and seas it is the womb of life. Share of my water and know that as the clouds, it is the seeker, the traveler with a mission. I share of the water, and may all know that as the streams and rivers, it is the shape changer, the destroyer of old, and at the same time, through change,*

the creatrix of new. Knowing well that water is the essence
of life, we have shared and become one, and now as one
we offer our lives to she who is the Mother of All Life,
in service and in love."

Faerie Faith is a mystical Path. As such, it has its own mysteries connected to the Beth-Luis-Nion system, as well as Shamanic mysteries that are part of any mystical Path.

CONTACT

E-mail: Clifflandis@hotmail.com

FURTHER READING

The Mabinogion, translated by Gwyn and Thomas Jones

draknetfree.com/clifflandis/
   Cliff's Faerie Faith Page.

home.earthlink.net/~irainey/
   The Hazel Nut.

www.faeriefaith.net/
   Linda Kerr's Faerie Faith Page.

www.geocities.com/mcfdianic/
   The McFarland Dianic home page.

www.witchvox.com/trads/trad_faerie.html

ABOUT THE CONTRIBUTOR

As of this writing, Cliff Landis is a 2nd Solar Student of the Faerie Faith. He recently graduated cum laude with a B.A. in Philosophy, with a concentration in Religious Studies, from Auburn University. His undergraduate thesis, "The Faerie Faith and the Beth-Luis-Nion System of the Celtic Lunar Tree Calendar," was published by Auburn University in May of 2002, in partial completion of his title as University Honors Scholar.

FERI TRADITION: VICIA LINE
By Phoenix Willow

Feri is an initiatory Tradition of Witchcraft emphasizing, to quote Cora Anderson in *Fifty Years in the Feri Tradition*, "the more natural and wild forms of human magic and sorcery." It contains a multiplicity of initiatory lineages, or *lines*, all ultimately tracing back to Victor and Cora Anderson. The Tradition's name has been spelled in a variety of ways over time. Early Initiates used Fairy, Faery, or Faerie, but Victor Anderson later changed the spelling to Feri in order to distinguish our Tradition from others using similar names.

Feri is an oral Tradition with no canonical book of rituals and lore. It also places a high value on poetic creativity and individual exploration. This has naturally led to variations between the practices of different lines. What follows is an outline of Feri as it is known and practiced in the Vicia line (pronounced *vee-chee-ah*.). In Vicia, we work with a body of material taught by Victor and Cora Anderson to their direct Initiates, primarily during the last decade of Victor's life. According to the Andersons, Vicia was also a very early name for the Feri Tradition.

According to Victor, Feri is a magical science that was practiced by a small dark-skinned people who came out of Africa tens of thousands of years ago. These are the original Fairy Folk or Little People, and they turn up in the legends of many cultures under different names. The Fairies were reputed to be strongly psychic and highly skilled in the magical arts. Victor considered himself a direct descendent of these small dark people and used to say, "I was not converted, I am kin to the Fairy race!" Because the Fairy Folk traveled so widely and lived so long ago, there are echoes of Feri to be found in practically every culture. (Some Feri Witches see this as a poetic explanation; others see it as literally true.)

In the late 1950s and early 1960s, the Andersons had "brought in," or initiated, several people. One was Gwydion Pendderwen (Tom DeLong), a young man who was a friend of their son. Gwydion went on to become a major contributor to the developing direction of the Tradition. Some Initiates, particularly those of Gwydion's direct lineage, consider him a cofounder of the Feri Tradition.

An important belief in Vicia is that the gods are not psychological constructs or inspirational ideas, but actual beings. Not only that, we are all part of a single family of evolving consciousness. There's a Feri maxim that states, "God is self and self is God, and God is a person like myself." In Vicia, our ultimate destiny is seen to be joining the company of gods. This work is usually accomplished over the course of many lifetimes. It is not seen as an easy or safe path to follow, but as Victor said many times, "Everything worthwhile is dangerous."

Polynesian religion and magic have been a major influence in Vicia. Other influences include Haitian Vodou, Kabbala, Native American concepts, European folk magic, and Gaelic lore. This is not mere eclecticism, but an acknowledgement of an underlying vision of reality to be found in many cultures. In Vicia, we have a strong code of ethics. At all times we are encouraged to have a high regard both for ourselves and for others. All humans are seen as kin—our brothers and sisters. We treat them with respect and love, and demand respect in return. We continually work to be in right relationship with the gods and each other. We are expected to help our brothers and sisters in the Craft when they are in need. We are also expected not to "coddle weakness" in ourselves or in others.

Some of the key principles of Vicia are embodied in the Feri Star or Decagram. The points of this 10-pointed star represent: Love, Wisdom, Knowledge, Law, Liberty, Sex, Self, Passion, Pride, and Power. Balance is sought in each point and between all of the points. A person who has achieved this balance is said to be "on their points." Ethical actions are a natural outgrowth of this state. In addition, sexual ethics are very important in Vicia. Sex is seen as a sacred act, and we know that we share the power of creation with the gods. Sexuality is not seen as a game or treated lightly, and we honor the vows we take to each other as lovers or spouses. A state of sexual purity is sought, akin to the innocent sexuality of childhood. In the Vicia line, this state is known as the Black Heart of Innocence.

In worship, we work with a unique body of liturgy, spells, rituals, and techniques passed down from the Andersons to their direct Initiates and covenmates. Original lore is carefully preserved, but new material is also created. Creative inspiration is seen as a mark of close contact with divinity.

CONTACT

E-mail: phoenix_willow@earthlink.net

FURTHER READING

Being a Pagan: Druids, Wiccans, and Witches Today,
    edited by Ellen Evert Hopman
Fifty Years in the Feri Tradition by Cora Anderson
The Spiral Dance by Starhawk
Thorns of the Blood Rose by Victor H. Anderson
www.cog.org/wicca/trads/faery.html
www.faerywolf.com
www.feritradition.org
www.feritradition.org/Witcheye
    The e-zine *Witch Eye*.
www.lilithslantern.com/bookstore.htm
www.tombostudios.com

www.vicia.info
www.witchvox.com/passages/victoranderson.html
www.witchvox.com/trads/trad_ferivl.html

ABOUT THE CONTRIBUTOR

Phoenix Willow first met the Andersons in 1997. Her teachers, Kalessin and Jim Schutte, are Initiates of the Andersons. She was formally initiated into Vicia in June of 2002 and currently lives in Southern California.

GARDNERIAN TRADITION
By Sine Silverwing

Our Tradition is named after Gerald B. Gardner (1884–1964), a British civil servant who studied magic and many other things over the course of a long life. He knew and worked with many famous occultists, not the least of which was Aleister Crowley (1875–1947). Gardner agreed with Margaret Murray's (1865–1965) premise that what was considered folk magick in Great Britain and Celtic Europe was actually the battered remnants of the original pre-Roman and possibly pre-Celtic religion of western Europe. He was probably encouraged and possibly inspired by the publication of Charles G. Leland's work on reclaiming similar survivals in Tuscany and from within the culture of the Romans. Certain traditional practices had survived in Gardner's family, and he found others who had preserved similar survivals and shared his beliefs in the ancientry of this knowledge.

Probably basing the structure of his work on what he had learned in various magickal lodges, Gardner set about reinventing that ancient, ancestral religion. He had little to work with; he had to write a good deal of it himself. He borrowed appropriate work from other artists, most notably

Aleister Crowley and Rudyard Kipling, Queen Victoria's Poet Laureate. Gardner's High Priestess, Doreen Valiente (1922–2000) wrote much of the most well-known poetry, including the much-quoted Charge of the Goddess.

The core group grew slowly and in utter secrecy; Witchcraft was illegal in Britain at the time. When the Witchcraft Laws were replaced, in 1951, by the Fraudulent Mediums Act, Gerald Gardner went public. The rest is history.

Our core beliefs include balance, duality, and the Goddess and the God in equal partnership. We acknowledge the reality of life and death as necessary cycles: in order for life to endure, there must be death. If nothing ever died, we would be up to our ears in houseflies in no time flat. It is the physical nature of humans to cooperate and compete, love and hate, kill and nurture. Balance is the goal. The Rede is a guiding principle, not an iron-clad rule. The coven is the basis of all Gardnerian organization; the coven is our family, the High Priestess and High Priest are first among equals. We preserve the original work by Gerald and Doreen, with expansion and creativity encouraged, as long as the rootstock is preserved and the legacy is identified as such. Ritual is important, but fellowship is more so. We practice gender magic, rather than sex magic as such; everything in Gardnerian is arranged male to female, female to male.

Gardnerian covens are autonomous. Each coven has its own personality, and an individual who is an honest seeker may not fit in with group A, but may be enthusiastically welcomed into group B. Because the coven is a family, the process from meet-and-greet and the polling of the Elders to the invitation to be initiated is more like a courtship than a screening process. The consummation of the courtship is the initiation; that is the agreement by the postulant and the coven that they want to make the relationship permanent. This is a permanent relationship, make no mistake! Because of that, initiation is not offered lightly.

An honest seeker who is perceived to not be suitable for Gardnerian initiation may be shown other Paths, so that more exploration might be conducted.

Each initiated Gardnerian Wiccan is a priestess or a priest, with direct, personal, one-to-one access to the gods. There are no intermediaries. There is no laity in Gardnerian Wicca. The obvious result of that is that there are no "ministers," no pastors. The closest things to that role (advisor, confidant, counselor, etc.) are the High Priestess and the High Priest. Gardnerians relate to the High Priestess and the High Priest as first among equals, as well as, in a sense, Mom and Dad. They don't need to be older, but they are almost always more experienced in the Craft, and if a covener comes to them with a problem they can't handle, it is their responsibility to help the covener find a way to solve the problem, magickally or mundanely. But because of the high value we place on fellowship and the internal cohesiveness of the coven-as-family, any member of the group may turn to any other member and be confident of aid.

Gardnerianism is the Path that states that only a Witch can make a Witch; we hold this to be true for those of our Path: only a Gardnerian can make another Gardnerian. We believe in the physical passing on of power; that is one of the reasons why we keep records of our lineages—we remember where the power came from. Part of the equality of the sexes in Gardnerian is that a woman is initiated by a man, and a man by a woman.

Ethically speaking, the four pillars of a Witch's strength are the power to dare (courage), the power to will (determination), the power to know (willingness to learn), and the power to keep silent (a sense of privacy and respect for others). The most important, if they can be ranked at all, is the last: Witches must respect other people's right to choose their own faith, if we are to expect it for ourselves. It is not appropriate for a Witch to brag about her accomplishments or to flaunt her membership in the coven.

It is *never* appropriate to reveal another person's membership without their permission.

We do not believe in sin; we believe in karma. We deal with it according to the Wiccan Rede. The Rede is so simple it almost qualifies as a Zen koan, but it is too easy to understand. "An it harm none, do what you will." One of the lines of poetry that Gerald Gardner borrowed from Aleister Crowley for his Book of Shadows was "Keep pure your highest ideal; strive ever toward it." When that is taken along with the Rede, one realizes that, as humans, there is no way we can succeed at "harm none." We can only strive ever toward that ideal. The word *rede* is a thousand years old; in Saxon, it meant "advice." That's all the Wiccan Rede is: *advice*. It is not a commandment.

One of the most important single points of Gardnerian practice is the fact that we worship skyclad. That means that all one wears into the circle is jewelry. We are naked in our rites because one's clothing anchors one's mind to mundane matters. Skyclad practice works just as the concept of ritual robes does: it helps your mind shift gears, puts your consciousness into the magickal place where the power flows. Another reason why skyclad practice is a necessary part of Gardnerian practice is that being unclothed together helps to foster emotional intimacy among the coveners. Anyone who's been in an indoor circle with a dozen people knows that you can't help touching one another. None of it is sexual, but it is intensely intimate. The coven needs this connection between the members for us to function together seamlessly.

CONTACT

E-mail: shaktisine@aol.com

FURTHER READING

Triumph of the Moon by Ronald Hutton
The works of Charles Godfrey Leland
The works of Doreen Valiente
The works of Gerald B. Gardner
The works of Margaret Murray
The works of Raymond Buckland
www.witchvox.com/trads/trad_gardnerian.html

ABOUT THE CONTRIBUTOR

Sine is a Third Degree Gardnerian priestess, initiated 16 years ago, and an Elder in Silver Star Coven. She works for her home county's department of social services and is openly Wiccan at work. She has been an occult and minorities religion consultant to local police and social services. She lives in western New York State on three acres of land, with coyotes, wild turkeys, and white-tailed deer competing for her produce and her attention.

GEORGIAN TRADITION
By Moondancer

A note from Trish: *I first learned of the Georgian Tradition through Dorothy Morrison, a popular author and great spokesperson for this Path. While her books do not directly discuss Georgian methods, the rich flavor of her writing provides a good feel for the ethics and attitudes of this group.*

The Georgian Tradition was founded in Bakersfield, California, in 1971, by George E. "Pat" Patterson III (1920–1984), Lady Persephone (now known as Zanoni), and Tanith.

These three were the High Priest, High Priestess, and Maiden of what was later known as the Persephone Coven (which was the original Georgian coven). Shortly thereafter, they incorporated as the Church of Wicca (adding "of Bakersfield," in order to distinguish from other "Churches of Wicca"). They were known by this name for several years, until they reincorporated in the late 1970s as "The Georgian Church," to serve as an umbrella for all of the covens of the Tradition, retaining the name "Church of Wicca of Bakersfield" as the permanent name for the "home coven."

Patterson, who stated that he originally received training from a group in the Boston area, drew on traditional material. Gardnerian and Alexandrian information expanded the core training material derived from an early version of Ed Fitch's *Grimoire of the Shadows*, along with material contributed by others in the United States and Great Britain, as well as Patterson's original writings in the development of the Georgian Tradition.

By 1973, there were several dozen Georgian covens—throughout California (mostly in the southern California area), Texas, Oregon, Washington, Oklahoma, New York, Florida, and elsewhere in the United States—and by 1980 there were Georgian groups in Europe. In order to keep up with the far-flung Tradition, the *Georgian Newsletter* was begun in 1974. Several persons who became nationally known wrote to and for this newsletter, including the late Ellen Cannon Reed. This chatty and informative newsletter, bringing news and useful hints for beginning from around the world, only missed one issue during the time that Pat was in charge of it, despite of his 24-hour on-call job and, later, in spite of the cancer that ultimately claimed his life.

Following Patterson's death in 1984, the main branch of the Tradition was led by Dean and Lady Fauna, who attempted to continue the *Georgian Newsletter*, but it ultimately ceased publication as a monthly and went first to an annual, then to infrequent publication. At present, it is no longer published in any form, although there have been discussions regarding a possible revival in one format or another. Dean passed away several years ago, and Lady Fauna largely withdrew from any public activity following that.

In 1975, representatives of two Georgian Covens (Church of Wicca of Bakersfield and the Sacred Grove of Vril) were present at the founding of Covenant of the Goddess (COG) in Oakland. Zanoni served on the initial Board of Directors, as a member at large; Moondancer served as national membership officer and held several offices at the local council level of COG, in both Southern California and Washington; and Lady Fauna served as an officer of the Southern California local Council for several years. Over the years, several Georgian covens and Initiates have given service to COG, both locally and nationally.

The Georgian Mountain Meet began as an annual camping event, in August of 1976, and continues as one of the oldest and long-running festivals in the United States. By the mid-1980s, thanks to computers, Georgians began to reconnect with each other. Several worked with the Pagan-Occult Distribution System, which aided many. Included in these efforts was anti-defamation activist Rowan Moonstone and author Dorothy Morrison. The Internet continued to be very valuable for networking, and various virtual groups formed, including one on Yahoo.

In terms of beliefs and philosophy, Georgian is a "blended" Tradition. Its Initiates have a light-hearted approach to the religious aspect as being celebratory of the life bestowed upon us, yet the Initiates are very serious in their approach to working for the help and healing of others. "Let there be mirth and reverence…" says the Charge of the Goddess, which Moondancer phrased as "taking our Craft seriously and ourselves not at all." Patterson's maxim was "if it works, use it—if it doesn't, find out why and find something that does."

MANIFESTO OF THE GEORGIANS

The aims and purposes of the Georgians shall be:

▶ To honor the Gods of the Old Religion.

▶ To aid the members to progress and improve themselves mentally, physically, and spiritually.

▶ To work magick for the benefit of members and any others who may seek out aid for right purposes.

▶ To aid others in learning the Craft who truly desire the knowledge of the Craft for proper reasons.

▶ To combat the untruths and to spread the truth about the Craft to those outside the Craft.

▶ To work for peace, harmony, and unity among the various branches of the Craft.

▶ To work for a better understanding of and a better relationship between man and nature.

Some of the key Georgian tenets and precepts include:

▶ The Georgian Tradition is normally taught and passed male to female, female to male.

▶ The Georgian Tradition is one of many branches of the Craft; it is traditional in that it is taught and passed generally through a coven setting and always by persons who have been initiated and elevated to the priesthood, according to the rites and rituals of the Tradition. It is eclectic in that it has origins in many sources: Alexandrian, Gardnerian, Celtic, and other Traditions, and values to a high degree the creativity and originality of its members.

▶ The Georgian Tradition is considered "oath-bound": the mysteries and lore of the Tradition are not passed to any but "proper persons" who have been "properly prepared."

▶ While the Internet is a useful tool in learning and communication, it does not provide a means for initiation or elevation to other degrees within the Georgian Tradition.

With regard to Deity, each coven establishes their own. Our tools are those commonly found in the British-derived Craft Traditions.

FURTHER READING

www.GeorgianWicca.org
This site also provides contacts.

ABOUT THE CONTRIBUTOR

Moondancer was originally initiated into the Georgian Tradition in Bakersfield, California, by Lord Scorpio (the late George Patterson) and Lady Aphrodite, at Beltane 1973. Her elevations were performed by Lady Persephone/ Zanoni Silverknife over the next few years. While she still has a certain fondness for the Georgian Tradition and, until recently, served as the group's Webmaster and e-mail list coordinator, she hasn't worked in the Tradition for nearly 25 years. She is an Elder High Priestess in the New England Covens of Traditionalist Witches (NECTW) and has worked within it or one of its related branches most of

the time since 1976. In 1975, she was one of the several
cofounders of Covenant of the Goddess and has served
twice on its National Board of Directors, as well as held
several offices in the Southern California and Northwest
Local Councils.

GOLDEN DAWN
By John Michael Greer

The Golden Dawn magical Tradition comes out of a
secretive underworld of magical lodges in England, dating
back at least to the beginning of the 18th century and possibly further still. From the time of John Dee (1527–1608),
who is court astrologer to Queen Elizabeth I, English magicians had been working with the teachings of Renaissance high magic in new ways, developing a rich heritage
of magical theory and practice that reached full flower
with the coming of the Golden Dawn (GD).

The Hermetic Order of the Golden Dawn itself was
founded in 1888 by a small group of magicians headed by
William Wynn Westcott and Samuel Mathers. It was
among the first organizations in British society to admit
women and men on an equal basis, and some of the most
influential female magicians of the time—Moina Mathers,
Florence Farr, and Dion Fortune, among others—were
active members of the GD or its later offshoots. Aleister
Crowley, Dion Fortune, and Israel Regardie each published elements of the GD system in their writings.
Regardie's massive collection *The Golden Dawn*, published
in four volumes between 1937 and 1940, included most of
the Order's rituals and teachings, and made the Golden
Dawn system available to several generations of magicians
around the world.

At present, most Golden Dawn magicians are solitary practitioners, self-trained and self-initiated, making use of a growing collection of books on the system. There are also dozens of active Golden Dawn-based temples and lodges around the world, some with connections to the original Order and others created from the ground up. The Golden Dawn Tradition has become one of the most widely practiced systems of magic in the world, and has been a major source of inspiration and ideas to many other systems and Traditions as well.

The Golden Dawn Tradition is a system of intensive spiritual and magical development, not unlike the great Mystical Traditions of Asia. Golden Dawn magicians use ritual, meditation, exercises for the development of clairvoyance and other psychic abilities, and similar methods to achieve direct personal experience of the hidden, magical side of reality. Like the ancient Gnostics, whose teachings form one of the roots of the Golden Dawn system, Golden Dawn magicians aren't willing to settle for belief; they want to know.

The traditional rituals we utilize include oaths in which candidates for initiation bind themselves to maintain the traditional secrecy of the Order, study and practice the Golden Dawn teachings, cooperate with the temple officers, treat their fellow members in an ethical and respectful fashion, and use any magical powers they may attain to positive ends alone. These obligations represent the core standards of conduct in the Golden Dawn Tradition. While the need for secrecy has largely passed and some of the details of the old oaths no longer apply, the basic principles are still relevant. Because the oaths have been published (along with the rest of the ritual texts) in Regardie's *The Golden Dawn* and elsewhere, they can be readily used as a test for the validity of any person or group who claims to be part of the Golden Dawn Tradition.

CONTACT

E-mail: threelynx@earthlink.net

FURTHER READING

Circles of Power by John Michael Greer
  Covers Golden Dawn ritual magic.
Paths of Wisdom by John Michael Greer
  A handbook of Golden Dawn Cabalistic theory and
  practice.
Self-Initiation into the Golden Dawn Tradition by Chic
  and Sandra Tabatha Cicero
  An excellent practical handbook.
The Golden Dawn by Israel Regardie
  After whetting your appetite, this source provides
  the core material of the Tradition.
The Mystical Qabalah by Dion Fortune
  Provides a good basic overview with much of the
  system's theoretical basis.
The Tree of Life by Israel Regardie
  Provides a good basic overview with much of the
  system's theoretical basis.
www.witchvox.com/trads/trad_goldendawn.html

ABOUT THE CONTRIBUTOR

John Michael Greer has been a student and practitioner of Golden Dawn magic for a quarter-century. He is a student of geomancy and sacred geometry and serves on the Council of Archdruids in the Ancient Order of the Druids in America (AODA). His books on the subject include *Paths of Wisdom*, *Circles of Power*, and *Inside a Magical Lodge*, all available from Llewellyn Publications.

GREEN WITCHCRAFT
By Ann Moura

A note from Trish: *Ann Moura has to be one of the most charming and kind women I've met in recent years. She recently opened her home to me (basically a total stranger) and treated me like kin. To me, this is a very strong reflection of her Path manifesting in day-to-day life. Thank you again, Ann!*

Green Witchcraft is a family oral Tradition, which I learned from my mother, who learned from her mother. My grandmother was a noted healer in her region of Brazil and preferred to work magic with candles, herbs, the Wind, and the Power. People came to her from miles around for cures, charms, and spells. My mother preferred magical workings with candles, flowers, plants, the Wind, birds, and the Power.

Divination, spiritism, candle magics, Fairy interaction, and the recognition of the dual nature of the Divine as female and male, were all part of the heritage handed down to me. The Sabbats were integrated with mainstream religions and culture, but were *experienced* rather than celebrated with formatted rituals. The noting of the day as well as the activities were focused on the flow of Nature and the spiritual meaning of the time. I have taken this foundation of information and added to it my own focus and interests, with all revolving around communion and oneness with Nature and the Divine in Nature. My children have also done this, personalizing the Green Path to their own interests, and I encourage people to also take what they feel drawn to from this heritage and make it an expression of their own.

The Rules of Conduct for Green Witchcraft were repeatedly spoken to me by my mother, as she said they had been repeated to her by her mother. I have found that these Rules sum up the practice of the Craft without restricting the practitioner from the Power.

The five Rules are:

1. Be careful what you do.
2. Be careful who you trust.
3. Never use the Power to harm another, for what is sent comes back.
4. Never use the Power against someone who has the Power, for you both draw from the same well.
5. To use the Power, you must *feel* it in your heart and *know* it in your mind.

There are different ways of walking the Green Path. A person can be considered a member of a mainstream religion while being a worker of folk magics, thus gaining the social and cultural protection of going unnoticed and fitting in with social norms. A person can work with the powers, spirits, and entities of Nature without any religious connection, being more of an independent free spirit who is at one with Nature. And a person can recognize the Green Path as their religion through their union with the Goddess and the God in a dedication ritual.

Sometimes, one or the other might flow together, depending on the circumstances. A person might appear to be a folk magic worker, but actually be dedicated to the Goddess and the God. To me, this indicates a secret, double life that could capitalize on the sentimentality of Catholicism while keeping the Old Religion going. The word *Witch* was never used. Once in my youth, someone overheard me talking to a friend about a family activity and said that was what Witches do. When I asked my mother if we were Witches, she said, "We never name ourselves—others name us. Those who need us will find us." As an oral Tradition, the passing on of information was so casual and ordinary seeming to me, that it was not until placed in the context of outsiders that the differences between our practices and those of other people were made clear.

In terms of Deity, my mother and grandmother kept their private deities hidden, but worked publicly with Catholic saints. They were devotees of Saint Francis of the Little Birds and Saint Theresa of the Little Flowers, whom they could easily identify with the Lord of the Wild Wood and the Lady of Nature. But in the home, the Lady and the Lord of Nature were found in Bendis, the Thracian Goddess of the Dark Moon and Witches, who holds a twig in her hand to point the way to Underworld, and in Shiva, whose name means "beneficent" and who is recognizable today as the Lord of the Dance. My children have taken the core teachings and adapted these to the deities that appeal to them, one with an Egyptian pantheon, the other with a Celtic pantheon, yet both have also retained the traditional family deities. They are openly Pagan and I genuinely admire their courage, for while I am true to my heritage, I tend to be rather circumspect.

Our basic altar is set up (as the practitioner faces it) with the God image and/or materials on the right side, the Goddess image and/or materials on the left side, and something to symbolize both at the center. A *cingulum*—a red silk cord with knots placed on it to "take your measure"—is part of the initiation ritual. If desired, the cord can be woven with other cords signifying methods of practice: gold for magic-worker, red for Initiate, black for Dedicant.

With the Green Path, the initiation is an introduction of the practitioner to the Divine, asking for guidance and instruction in the Craft. The dedication occurs when the practitioner feels ready to open the channels of communication permanently. While this may happen spontaneously for some people, the ritual is a very moving experience, bringing the practitioner into direct contact with the Goddess and the God, with all the senses engaged. This is called an *ecstatic religious experience*, but a label does not do justice to this powerful encounter.

The Green Path is both animistic and pantheistic, meaning that everything is alive and the Divine is in everything. Thus, while the Goddess and the God are seen in balance as One, they are also seen as separate, aspected through the Elementals, and able to express themselves in any pantheon with any image that gets your attention and offers you a focus. Labels are simply too limiting for the Divine.

I have written rituals down in the *Green Witchcraft* series of books. Without repeating from these works, let me say that chants and prayers are spoken from the heart, as a conversation with an immanent Divine. This is like talking to someone standing right in front of you, connecting and communicating on a personal level, so each prayer and most chants are new and fresh. An example of a simple chant is this one for Hogmanay Eve (New Year's Eve):

> *Queen of the Moon*
> *King of the Sun*
> *Health, wealth, happiness be Thy boon*
> *To me throughout the New Year's run.*

CONTACT

Website: *www.annmourasgarden.com*

FURTHER READING

Green Magic: The Sacred Connection to Nature by Ann Moura
A more advanced book on the working of magic.

Green Witchcraft II: Balancing Light & Shadow by Ann Moura

Green Witchcraft III: The Manual by Ann Moura
Based on the course I teach once in a rare while that uses Green Witchcraft as the textbook.

Green Witchcraft: Folk Magic, Fairy Lore, and Herb Craft by Ann Moura

Grimoire for the Green Witch: A Complete Book of Shadows by Ann Moura
Duplicates my personal Book of Shadows and grimoire.

Tarot for the Green Witch by Ann Moura

GWYDDONIC ORDER
By Mairwen y Gwydd

The Gwyddonic Order was founded at Lughnassad 1998, when Mairwen y Gwydd separated her group (the College of the Blue Butterfly) from Trefn Gwyddoniad, an American-Welsh-Celtic Tradition based in Northern California. The Gwyddoniad is a Welsh-Celtic spiritual, philosophical, and metaphysical Tradition. Our philosophical foundation is Oneness: "Everything is the One, and the One is the All," meaning that nothing and no one is more or less the One than anything or anyone else.

We are Craft practitioners who follow strict teachings, certainly, but we are not Wiccans and do not call ourselves Witches or Druids. In the Gwyddonic Order, a male is a *gwyddon* (pronounced *gwih-thon*), and a female is a *gwiddon* (pronounced *gwie-thon*). A Third Degree Gwyddon is considered a High Priest.

The Gwyddonic Order has an ordered group structure. When a seeker is initiated, he is "born" into the Tuatha of Kerridwen (pronounced *too-ah-thah* of *ker-ihd-win* or *kuh-rid-win*); he becomes a member of our *tuatha*— our tribe, our family. The Gwyddonic Order is further divided into colleges. A college consists of at least three people—a High Priestess, a High Priest, and one member. A college can be no larger than 25 members. A college is the basic community structure in the Gwyddoniad. As the name implies, its main purpose is to teach. One of the main ways in which a college differs from a coven is its mutability; whereas a coven may practice for years with the same members, a college's main job is to train others in the Art and Craft so that they may start their own colleges.

The gods we worship are Irish, Gaelic, Welsh, and Teutonic. Worship is the love and rapport we establish with our gods. Our Greater Book of the Art and Craft has a list of 35 gods, and we have an optional expanded list of 78 gods. However, this doesn't mean we are limited to these gods. The Indo-European god family has more than 500 members. The Tuatha de Danaan, or Tribe of the Goddess D'Anu (pronounced *dan-oo* or *dah-noo*), the family members who are presently Gods, or humans who have transcended the physical limitations of their existence to become deity-like. D'Anu translates to "of the Great Mother." The Tuatha of Kerridwen are the family members who are presently human, incarnate here on Earth.

What we do as Gwyddons encompasses more as worship than as magic. Magic is secondary to the Gwyddon, whose goal is to know what he is and what Deity is. A seeker will notice that we do not have volumes of spellwork, nor do we have pages of instruction on spell construction.

A Gwyddon works through the Five Little Works (part of our teaching and part of the *Greater Book of the Art and Craft*) to learn Gwyddon methods of using magic. That's it. Our Little Works are methods. Not spells.

Some of the qualities that make a good college member are having an open mind and being willing to put forth the effort to learn. Our Tradition is a "tough" one; anyone on this path will tell you the same thing. We even have a disclaimer on our Website stating that this is not a path for "wimps." If a person doesn't put forth the effort, he goes nowhere. If he tries to "follow the path of himself" within this Tradition, he's turned away. What makes a good student is someone who's willing to let go of what he already thinks he knows in order to learn something new.

Once accepted into the Order, to progress, the student must ask for the "next step" of lessons, and to be elevated to the next level (or degree), he must petition his teacher. The teacher assigns certain studies and projects for the student to accomplish—but that accomplishment is totally up to the student. We don't "hand hold" our students/priests like some groups do. The only way a student can find himself and his Path is on his own.

The Gwyddonic Order is not in any way affiliated with or associated with Trefn Gwyddoniad/y Awenechen or with Y Tylwyth Teg. If you would like more information about The Gwyddonic Order, please feel to visit our Website.

CONTACT

Website: *www.gwyddoniad.org*
E-mail: mairwenhps@att.net (Mairwen y Gwydd)
    Gwyddoniad@gwyddoniad.org (The Gwyddonic Order)

FURTHER READING

www.witchvox.com/trads/trad_gwyddonic.html

ABOUT THE CONTRIBUTOR

Mairwen y Gwydd is a Gwyddon Elder and cofounder of the organization.

HAITIAN VODOU:
SERVING THE SPIRITS
By Michael Rock

A note from Trish: *This article had to be edited dramatically due to space constraints. Please contact Michael and read his write-up on witchvox (see the link in Further Reading) to get a far more complete picture of Haitian Vodou than could be provided in this abbreviated version.*

Haitian Vodou, called *Sevis Giné* (African Service), is the primary culture and religion of the approximately 7 million people of Haiti and the Haitian diaspora. It has its primary roots among the Fon-Ewe peoples of West Africa, in the country now known as Benin, formerly the Kingdom of Dahomey. It also has strong elements from the Ibo and Kongo peoples of Central Africa and the Yoruba of Nigeria, though many different peoples or "nations" of Africa have representation in the liturgy of the Sevis Giné, as do the Tainos—the original peoples of the island we now know as Hispaniola. Haitian Vodou exists in Haiti, the Dominican Republic, parts of Cuba, the United States, France, Montreal, and other places that Haitian immigrants have dispersed to over the years.

Haitian Vodou came to the United States to a significant degree beginning in the late 1960s and early 1970s with the waves of Haitian immigrants under the oppressive Duvalier regime, taking root in Miami, New York City, Chicago, and other cities, mainly on the two coasts.

Vodouisants believe, in accordance with widespread African tradition, that there is one God who is the creator of all, referred to as *Bondje*, from the French words *Bon Dieu*, meaning "Good God." Bondje is distant from his/her/its creation though, and so it is the spirits or the mysteries, saints, or angels that the Vodouisant turns to for help, as well as to the ancestors. The Vodouisant worships God and serves the spirits, who are treated with honor and respect as elder members of a household might be. There are said to be 21 nations or *nanchons* of spirits, also sometimes called *lwa-yo*.

In Vodou, spirits are divided according to their nature, into roughly two categories, whether they are hot or cool. Cool spirits fall under the Rada category, and hot spirits fall under the Petwo category. Rada spirits are familial and mostly come from Africa; Petwo spirits are mostly native to Haiti and are more demanding and require more attention to detail than the Rada, but both can be dangerous if angry or upset. Neither is "good" or "evil" in relation to the other.

Everyone has spirits, and each person has a special relationship with one particular spirit who is said to "own their head." However, each person may have many lwa, and the one that owns their head, or the *met tet*, may or may not be the most active spirit in a person's life.

In serving the spirits, Vodouisants seek to achieve harmony with their own individual natures and the world around them, manifested as personal power and resourcefulness in dealing with life. Part of this harmony is membership in and maintaining relationships within the context of family and community. A Vodou house or society is organized on the metaphor of an extended family, and Initiates are the "children" of their initiators, with the sense of hierarchy and mutual obligation that implies.

Most Vodouisants are not initiated and are referred to as being *bosal*; it is not a requirement to be an Initiate in order to serve one's spirits. There are clergy in Vodou whose responsibility it is to preserve the rituals and songs and maintain the relationship between the spirits and the community as a whole (though some of this is the responsibility of the whole community as well). They are entrusted with leading the service of all of the spirits of their lineage.

The cultural values that Vodou embraces center around ideas of honor and respect—to God, to the spirits, to the family and *sosyete* (society), and to oneself. There is a plural idea of proper and improper, in the sense that what is appropriate to someone with a Danbala as their head may be different from someone with an Ogou as their head, for example—one spirit is very cool and the other one is very hot. I would say that coolness, overall, is valued and so is the ability and inclination to protect oneself and one's own if necessary. Love and support within the family of the Vodou sosyete seems to be the most important consideration. Generosity in giving to the community and to the poor is also an important value. Our blessings come to us through our community, and we should be willing to give back to it in turn. Because Vodou has such a community orientation, there are no solitaries in Vodou—only people separated geographically from their Elders and house. It is not a "do it yourself" religion—a person without a relationship of some kind with Elders will not be practicing Vodou. You can't pick the fruit if you don't start with a root.

Initiation in Haitian Vodou is a serious matter, and it is *not* advised to run off to Haiti with the first person you encounter on the internet or elsewhere, sight unseen or otherwise, who says they will initiate you. Take the time to get to know your prospective Maman or Papa in the Vodou, and the members of their society. Attend ceremonies in person, ask questions, learn, check references. Serve your ancestors, cultivate patience, and wait. Pay attention to dreams or other messages from the spirits. Haitian Vodou does not proselytize and it is not for sale, although even valid initiations do cost some money, due to the time, people, materials, and travel involved

Initiate or not, once you belong to a house and have chosen an Elder, it is important to follow the guidance they provide as to the way things are done in their house, called the *Regleman Giné*. Although the general structure of ritual and practice are the same across Haiti, small details of service and the spirits served will vary from house to house, and information in books or on the Internet may be contradictory. When in doubt, etiquette dictates that one consult their own Maman or Papa in the Vodou, and practice as they direct according to the regleman of their lineage, because "every manbo and houngan is the head of their own house," according to a common saying in Haiti taught to me by Houngan Aboudja.

This is the most basic overview of the Haitian Vodou religion imaginable, keeping in mind that I am by no means an expert (compared to my Elders) after only a couple of years in the religion as an hounsi. Vodou is not a religion limited by race or ethnicity, because ultimately, as science has proven, we are *all* the children of Africa, and the waters of Giné join us all.

CONTACT

Website: *www.Mike-Rock.com*
   Michael Rock's Website, with e-mail links provided.

FURTHER READING

Island Possessed by Katherine Dunham

Mama Lola: A Vodou Priestess in Brooklyn by Karen
    McCarthy Brown

Sacred Arts of Haitian Vodou by Donald Cosentino

alt.religion.orisha

alt.religion.voodoo

groups.yahoo.com/group/tristatevodou
    Tristate Vodou.

groups.yahoo.com/group/vodouspirit
    Vodouspirit.

haitiforever.com/windowsonhaiti/welcome.html
    Windows on Haiti.

soc.culture.haiti

www.amnh.org/exhibitions/vodou/
    Sacred arts of Haitian Vodou.

www.cia.gov/cia/publications/factbook/geos/ha.html
    CIA World Factbook, Haiti.

www.ethnocool.com
    Danse Adje.

www.everythinghaitian.com
    Everything Haitian.

www.luckymojo.com
    Lucky Mojo Curio Co.

www.vodou.org
    The temple of Yewe—Peristyle Mariani.

www.vodoun.com
    Vodou Culture.

www.vodouspirit.com
    Flower of Abomey Society of Haitian Vodou in New
    Orleans.

www.voodoospiritualtemple.org
    Priestess Miriam Chamani.

www.witchvox.com/words/words_2002/e_samhain05.html
    An Ancestor Novena by Steven Bragg.
yorubapriestess.tripod.com
    Priestess Ava Kay Jones.

ABOUT THE CONTRIBUTOR

Michael Rock is a poet, artist, folk magician, herbalist, spiritualist, Witch, and philosopher. Michael finds inspiration in Haitian Vodou, Asian spiritualities, indigenous lifeways, Faery, Chaos Magic, Discordianism, Science Fiction, Gnostic Christianity, Roman Catholicism, European Witchcraft, Mediterranean, Celtic and Germanic Paganisms, and other streams of wisdom, ancient and modern. He is a "hounsi lave tet" or "hounsi kanzwe" Initiate of the Flower of Abomey Society of Haitian Vodou based in New Orleans, Louisianna. Michael has a passion for the Faery Pentagrams of Iron and Pearl, for song and chant, and for astronomical esoterica. He remains active in the Reclaiming Tradition of Witchcraft with Tejas Web (*Tejasweb.org*) where he uses technology to weave community. Visit him on the World Wide Web at *www.Mike-Rock.com*.

HEATHEN (GERMANIC PAGANISM)
By Karen of Mercian Heathen Hearth

The Heathen "revival" started during the late 19th century, with people taking an interest in runes as well as Norse and Germanic history and mythology. A few Heathen groups did form in Germany, but most did not survive the Nazis either directly (they were outlawed) or after the war because of the misappropriation of their symbols by the Nazis. It wasn't until the 1960s that people began looking at Heathenry again and groups formed independently of each other in Iceland, Germany, the United Kingdom, and the United States. Some of these are still going today, and others have disappeared or evolved into other groups. The main UK group was the Odinic Rite, which is still going.

Now, as in the past, a lot of Heathenry is based on local communities. There isn't a single form of Heathenry, and Heathens in the United Kingdom are different from those in Iceland, who are also different from those in the United States. I'd say some of the most important UK figures are those who promote Heathenry (we're not very big on "leadership"), such as Jenny Blain; Math Jones, who runs Midgard's Web; Thorskegga and Dragon of the Thorshof, who knock themselves out to provide workshops and talks all over the place; and Arlea and Stormerne Hunt-Anschutz, who are a mine of information to pretty much anyone who asks them.

Heathenry is Germanic Paganism. One of the most widely quoted "ethical" systems in Heathenry is the Nine Noble Virtues—Courage, Discipline, Fidelity, Honour, Hospitality, Industriousness, Perseverance, Self-Reliance, and Truthfulness—but these are a modern guideline to help Heathens remember how our ancestors were expected to behave according to the Eddas and Sagas. Most Heathens adopt these virtues or a similar code (it's certainly easier to remember than the Sagas!).

In our Tradition, *Wyrd* is the force that flows through the universe—it is a system of cause and effect and each Heathen has to recognize that their action (or inaction) has a set of probable or possible consequences. It is not a system of punishment and reward. It is also not monitored by divine powers—indeed, the gods are as subject to Wyrd as we are. Heathenry is also very much concerned with life as we live it rather than the promise of a wonderful (or terrible) afterlife or reincarnation. Heathens do believe in an afterlife but it is not the focus of our beliefs.

A large part of Heathenry centers on honoring our ancestors and wights (spirits that cannot be perceived on a mundane level equivalent to brownies, faeries, lares, and so on). Ancestors can be your literal ancestors or "cultural ancestors," such as King Penda who was a Heathen ruler of the kingdom of Mercia or, say, Lord Nelson, who ensured I wouldn't have to type this in French!

In Heathenry, oath-taking is a very serious business! The good news is that the vast majority of oaths are those of loyalty rather than secrecy. The two main rituals are the *blot* (pronounced *bloat*) and the *symbel* (pronounced *sumbel*). To blot is to make an offering to an appropriate recipient—this can be a god, ancestor, or wight—and blots can be offerings to many beings at once. It is most common to make an offering of food or drink that is either thrown onto a fire, tipped onto the earth, or left in an appropriate place. Other offerings include poetry and music. Sadly, as we often blot in parks or common ground, part of our offering often consists of taking away litter that others have left behind.

A symbel is a round of toasts and sometimes boasts, done in a ritual manner. The first round is often to the gods, the second to the ancestors, and the third to the wights. It may stop there or can continue for a set number of rounds—or until you run out of mead. A boast may take the form of "I have done" or "I am going to." If the latter, you *must* act upon it—the gods are listening.

FURTHER READING

groups.yahoo.com/group/ukheathenry
www.bbc.co.uk/religion/religions/paganism/subdivisions/
    heathen.shtml
www.midgard.pwp.blueyonder.co.uk/heathen/

www.midgardsweb.f2s.com/
www.thorshof.org
www.wyrdwords.vispa.com/heathenry

HELLENISM
(HELLENIC ETHNIC TRADITION)
By Kresphontes

Hellenism (Hellinikos Ethnismos), an ancient indigenous Tradition, was born and evolved in Hellas (Greece) as a religion and cosmotheory. It is a certain form of human consciousness and an everyday ethos, and it is the most well-documented of the ancient polytheistic nature-religions. Its core principles may be summed up in these words: Dignity, Freedom, Beauty, Honesty, Variety, Tolerance, and Candor.

Hellenism perceives Cosmos (*Kosmos*, that is, the Universe) as an ever-existing being, which not only was not created by some "creator" God out of nothing, but on the contrary, allowed the Gods themselves to be created through its procedures. Hellenism understands Cosmos as *Apeiron* (Infinity) in great, wonderful order and therefore, in Hellenic language, Cosmos means also "jewel" (Kosmos, Kosmema). In the Hellenic Cosmotheory, the laws are:

- ▶ *Antipeponthos*: Roughly meaning "all events influence others," though without "cause and effect."
- ▶ *Nomos*: The entirety of the universal physical laws.
- ▶ *Anagke*: Need and fate, which all Gods respect and obey.

The Hellenic perception of *Chronos* (Time) is not linear, nor circular, but spiral. Through this shape of Time, the annual circles, the lunar circles, the human (and all) life, and the art of prophecy, are fully interpreted.

No dualism of "good and evil" exists in the Immortal Cosmos. We become virtuous only because we choose to be such. Hellenism also honors and worships conscious forces and energies alongside abstract ideas such as harmony, justice, freedom, and beauty. These ideas are alive— they have form and consciousness.

The "male" and "female" terms inside the Hellenic pantheon have nothing to do with the sexism and dualism dwelling in the minds of followers of other cultures. *Our Gods have no genitals.* The existence of six gods and six goddesses inside the Hellenic pantheon only serves to declare the total balance of all elements and characteristics inside the Sphere of Cosmos. Additionally, philosophy (which means "lover of wisdom or truth") is an inseparable part of Hellenic Tradition and everyone who follows this tradition must study and *learn* what philosophy is and *use* it for her or his evolution and understanding of Divine/Cosmic laws.

There are several organizations or groups (mostly in Greece) that are autonomous, and since 1997, an organization (Supreme Council of the Gentile Hellenes, or SCGH) was founded, aiming to defend, study, and restore the ethnic, polytheistic Hellenic Tradition, religion, and way in contemporary Greek society. SCGH is a founding member of the World Congress of Ethnic Religions (WCER), which supports equal representation and value for distinctive people and religions. WCER's motto is "Unity in Diversity" and is categorically opposed to discrimination, suppression, or persecution based on race, color, social class, religion, or national origin.

CONTACT

E-mail: ysee@ysee.gr

FURTHER READING

(Please note that you may have to use a translation program on some of these sites or click on "English" version.)

www.geocities.com/kresphontes.geo/
www.wcer.org/
www.witchvox.com/trads/trad_hellenism.html
www.ysee.gr/

ABOUT THE CONTRIBUTOR

Kresphontes lives in Greece and has been a member of the ÕÓÅÅ (in English, the SCGH—Supreme Council of the Gentile Hellenes) since its inception.

HOLY ORDER OF MOTHER EARTH (HOME)
By Oberon Zell-Ravenheart

The Holy Order of Mother Earth (HOME) was founded by Morning Glory and Oberon Zell, Anna Korn, and Alison Harlow and chartered in 1978 as a Magickal Order of the Church of All Worlds (CAW). Rituals have been developed over 20 years of living and working on sacred lands in Northern California, and threads were woven in from the various other Traditions that members of the rural homesteading community had been trained in: CAW, Faerie, Dianic, Strega, Shamanic, Celtic, New Reformed Orthodox Order of the Golden Dawn (NROOGD), Mohsian, and so on.

Most of the HOME rituals are designed for large groups (30 to 100), and tend towards Mystery Pageants, all-night vigils, and "bardics" (much HOME liturgy takes the form of songs and chants). Practices are basically Shamanic, and the thealogy is CAW/Gaean. Our mythological basis is primarily British and Greek (though particular rituals may encompass other mythologies as well, such as Sumerian, Egyptian, or Welsh), and the eight-Sabbat Wheel of the Year combines the May Cycle and the Eleusinia. Rituals are seldom repeated, but usually created fresh for each occasion. A basic liturgy, however, has been compiled in a "Magick 101" course and a three-volume *HOME Cooking.* (*HOME Cooking, Book I,* is now available for $12 plus $1 postage. It contains 66 pages, in a hard loose-leaf binder. Order from HOME, P.O. Box 688, Penngrove, CA 94951.)

HOME joined the Covenant of the Goddess as a charter member in 1979, and participated actively in organizational meetings from Los Angeles to Seattle, as well as the local NorCal CoG Council. The original envisioned purpose of HOME "of establishing and maintaining a wilderness sanctuary and religious retreat/training center" had to be tabled until we could obtain land to support such a dream. However, our unique HOME Tradition continued to be the unifying designation for the rites and rituals we had developed

A "Branch Description" of HOME, dated March 28, 1992, listed HOME's purpose as being "responsible for making the CAW vision real through well conducted and appropriate rituals and festivals." Responsibilities of HOME included ensuring that each Sabbat, festival, or other ritual occasion is properly scheduled, staged, promoted, and staffed; keeping a library of ritual scripts; and assembling guidelines for rituals, overall outreach, and coordination of clergy.

Basically, HOME is polytheistic and also pantheistic. We accept and occasionally invoke deities from any of the world's many pantheons that may appeal to us at a particular time and circumstance—particularly at *Walpurgisnacht* (May Eve), which has commonly been the occasion for a group journey into other realms.

Here's our traditional CAW/HOME food blessing, written by Moonrose in the early 1980s:

Holy Mother Earth, yours is the power

To grow, to destroy, to give birth.
We conjure you now:

By seed and by shoot; by flower and fruit;

By light and by love; from below and above.

In Your ancient names:
Koré, Demeter, Persephoné.

Grant us the blessings of your body;

Thank you for the blessings of your body!

I intend, eventually, to have a Website dedicated to the Church of All Worlds Tradition, which will make available to everyone the 40 years' worth of good stuff we conceived and created when CAW was a Pagan religion and a "congregational" church. I am also embedding the best of CAW and HOME philosophy, rituals, and teachings, as appropriate, into the books—one of which just came out: *Grimoire for the Apprentice Wizard* (New Page Books, 2004). You can also read a great deal about the true and original CAW in the books listed in the Further Reading section.

CONTACT

www.mythicimages.com/Oberon.html
> The HOME magickal Tradition and the liturgy we developed therein is still my practice, so you can visit my professional Website for our statuary and e-mail me if you have questions.

FURTHER READING

Drawing Down the Moon by Margot Adler
Encyclopedia of Witches and Witchcraft by Rosemary Guiley

ABOUT THE CONTRIBUTOR

Oberon Zell-Ravenheart is an Elder in the worldwide magickal community. In 1962, he cofounded the Church of All Worlds, a Pagan church with a futuristic vision, and has been involved in founding several other groups and alliances. First to apply the terms *Pagan* and *Neo-Pagan* to the newly emerging Nature Religions of the 1960s, and through the publication of *Green Egg* from 1968–2000, Oberon was instrumental in the coalescence of the modern Pagan movement. In 1970, he had a profound vision of the Living Earth, and published an early version of *The Gaia Thesis*. Oberon is the primary artist for the Mythi Images Collection, and his first book, *Grimoire for the Apprentice Wizard* (New Page Books), was just released to bookstores. Oberon lives in Northern California with his lifemate Morning Glory and senior members of the Ravenheart Family.

KELTRIAN DRUIDISM
By Tony Taylor

A note from Trish: *Please note point 13 in this essay, as the idea of "living faith" is very common in Neo-Paganism. There is an underlying sense that beliefs must grow and adjust with humankind's ongoing growth and the world's transformations.*

Keltrian Druidism was founded in 1985, by members of Ár nDraíocht Féin who were looking for a Celtic-specific path. In doing so, they built an organization, The Henge of Keltria, and a Tradition honoring our ancestors, revering the spirits of nature, and worshipping the gods and goddesses of our Celtic heritage. The Tradition uses a very specific formula in its ritual form. Those people who regularly practice Keltrian-style ritual and who define themselves as Keltrian Druids are following the Tradition, regardless of their membership within The Henge of Keltria. There are groves and study groups in several states.

Keltrian Druids have developed 13 statements, which encompass their values and world view. We believe:

1. Divinity, as it is manifest in the Celtic pantheons, and that polytheism, pantheism, panentheism, animism, and pan-polytheism are all valid theistic perceptions of the pantheon.
2. That nature is the embodiment of the gods.
3. That natural law reflects the will of the gods.
4. That all life is sacred and should be neither harmed nor taken, without deliberation or regard.
5. In the immortality of the spirit.
6. That our purpose is to gain wisdom through experience, and that we may undergo several

incarnations to facilitate the variety of experience necessary to gain wisdom.

7. That learning is an ongoing process, and should be encouraged at all ages.

8. That morality is a matter of personal conviction, based on self-respect and respect for others.

9. Evil is not a matter of inheritance but of intent. Actions are not, in themselves, evil. Rather, it is through the intent behind actions that evil manifests.

10. In the relative nature of all things. Nothing is absolute, and all things, even the gods, have their dark sides.

11. That every individual has the right to pursue knowledge and wisdom through his or her chosen Path.

12. In honoring the gods through the cyclical celebrations of our Celtic ancestors.

13. In a living religion, able to adapt to a changing environment. Therefore, we recognize that our beliefs may undergo change as our Tradition grows.

Besides the 13 beliefs, there are the three foundations, which are to:

1. Honor the ancestors.

2. Revere the Nature Spirits.

3. Worship the gods and goddesses of our Celtic tribe.

All religious activities of Keltrian Druids should be directed to support one of those three foundations.

Our groups are organized into *groves*. Keltrian groves must abide by the Henge beliefs, ethics, bylaws, and religious methodology. Chartered groves apply to the Henge of

Keltria Board of Trustees and are granted charter pursuant to a recommendation of the Council of Elders. There are differing terms for a grove, based upon the achievement level of the grove leader. Groups who are just beginning may register themselves as study groups. Study groups may be practicing Keltrian Druidism and have all the appearances of being a grove but have not formally gone through the chartering process. Finally, there are many individuals who are practicing Keltrian Druid Ritual in a solitary environment. They may meet with one or more other individuals, on occasion, and may appear to be study groups but have not registered themselves as such.

Members of The Henge of Keltria are bound by the bylaws of the organization, which includes a set of ethical requirements. These ethical rules are similar to most Neo-Pagan organizations and include the following:

1. Shall not discriminate on the basis of age, race, color, national origin, sex, or sexual preference.

2. Shall not espouse or engage in the practice of blood sacrifice.

3. Shall not participate in the torture, mutilation, enslavement, or abuse (physical or emotional) of any sentient creature.

4. Clergy are expected to be honest, to abide by the law, respect the rights and privacy of others, to maintain a professional profile, and to respect certain sexual taboos placed upon virtually all professionals in our society, rules which have been instituted for the protection of the client.

Because we consider ourselves a nature religion, the ideal place for our rituals is outdoors, preferably in the woods or another place away from cities and "civilization." This is not always practical, especially during winter, so we worship wherever it is convenient. The purpose of our rituals is to celebrate the Divine and have communion with the gods and each other. We do this mainly through meditation, prayer, and invocation of the gods, ancestors, and Nature Spirits.

Most of our rituals are done around a sacred fire (or sacred candles, for indoor rituals). Our rituals involve the participation of everyone in attendance. We distribute the ritual functions among several people, rather than have everything done by a priest and priestess. Our rituals also involve the participants through a good deal of singing and dancing.

Through our rites, we relate the cycle of the year to the cycle of our lives. We choose a specific God and Goddess (Patron and Matron) to honor at each rite. These deities represent a different aspect of our lives, from youth to vitality to old age, wisdom, and finally death. As the year gets older, the Patron and Matron age as well.

In addition to the eight feasts, we celebrate two lunar rites. They are called the Mistletoe Rite and the Vervain Rite. The ancient Druids collected mistletoe on the sixth night of the moon (roughly just before the first quarter). Because mistletoe was known as "all heal," one of the themes of this rite is healing. This theme extends to healing of our community, through a sharing of food and drink at the rite. The sun and moon are in a position of equilibrium at this time, so we also see this as a time of balance. This is when we seek to find balance in our lives.

Our other lunar rite is the Vervain Rite. The time of this rite was also chosen from classical descriptions of ancient Druidic practices. It was written that vervain was gathered when neither sun nor moon were in the sky. (This occurs sometime during each night, except when the moon is full.) We generally celebrate this around the third quarter. This gives ample time for the rite during the evening hours. It also places this rite opposite the Mistletoe Rite in the lunar cycle. Vervain is said to be of aid in working magic. Thus, the Vervain Rite is our time for working magic. The purpose of magic, in a Druidic sense, is more like prayer. We work magic to help effect change in our lives. Druidic magic may involve contemplation, meditation, ritual, or ecstatic dance.

CONTACT
E-mail: Keltria-Office@keltria.org

FURTHER READING

The By-Laws of The Henge of Keltria
    Available online at *www.keltria.org/Bylaws.htm.*
The Henge of Keltria Book of Ritual by The Henge of Keltria
    Available online at *www.keltria.org/membersh.htm.*
The Henge: An Introduction to Keltrian Druidism by The Henge of Keltria
    Available online at *www.keltria.org/membersh.htm.*
www.keltria.org
www.keltria.org/druidq3.htm
    "What is The Henge of Keltria & What is Neopagan Druidism?"
www.witchvox.com/trads/trad_keltriandruidism.html

KITCHEN WITCHCRAFT
By Trish Telesco

Kitchen Witchery is known by many names, including *hearth magick* and *folk magick*. It is perhaps the oldest known Tradition in magickal circles, as it sprang from the hearts and lives of everyday people, in simple and beautiful ways. Our ancestors built the fireplace of any home first, as it was the heart of the dwelling. Here, to this very day, people gather to tell their stories, share of their news, and commune with those they love. So the hearth of the matter in Kitchen Witchery is the sacred space of home! This is also from where the Kitchen Witch gets her components and tools.

Simplicity, creativity, and personalization are the three legs on which Kitchen Magick has always stood. Kitchen Witches do not buy into the "fancy is better" outlook of modern society. Rather, in this practice, life is the act of worship, our bodies the Temple, and everything else you can bring to that becomes proverbial icing on the cake. Here's a great poem that sums it up nicely:

Kitchen Witch ABC's by Jeannette Lynn

Always stir in a clockwise motion;
Before you chop veggies, offer thanks;

Cut mindfully, thankfully;
Do all preparations in a loving spirit;

Energize food with good thoughts;
Feast gratefully;

Give and share what you can spare;
Home and hearth are sacred;

Invoke blessings of Goddess on all food;
Join hands with friends often;

Kindness shows in serving food;
Love goes into every dish;

Mindfully gather ingredients; No wasting—
recycle, compost, feed animals;

Open your senses, enjoy your surroundings;
Play as well as work;

Quench thirst, thinking of clear clean rivers;
Resolve to be grateful and waste not;

*Salivate as you smell fragrance
and anticipate flavors;*

Thank the universe and Goddess for health;

*Use utensils carefully, then clean up;
Value time spent with loved ones;*

*When possible, grow and harvest your food;
Xtra food is for creative recombining;*

*Yearly rituals and feasts build traditions;
Zestful living in every area is our goal.*

Similar to Eclectic Wicca and Paganism, the Kitchen Witch stays true to his or her principles and vision, while reconnecting with the Hearth God and Goddess within and without. Frugality, functionality, finesse, and fun are all sacraments to us. And while we call ourselves Kitchen Witches, our practice certainly isn't limited to the kitchen! In fact, so limiting our Craft goes against everything for which the Kitchen Witch strives—namely, living and being the magick every moment of every day.

Exactly what form this takes in each Kitchen Witch's life varies according to his or her needs and circumstances. I find myself working magick into everything from doing laundry to cooking (okay, especially cooking!). It gives "you are what you eat" a whole new meaning! In a world where many people are already multitasking to the maximum, this makes Kitchen Witchery very appealing; it combines the mundane with the spiritual in very effective ways.

CONTACT

Website: *www.loresinger.com*
   Trish Telesco's home page.

FURTHER READING

Any of these books of mine can get you started, as well as the useful Websites that follow:

Bubble-Bubble-Toil-and-Trouble
A Charmed Life
Kitchen Witch's Companion
    Forthcoming from Kensington/Citadel.
Kitchen Witch's Cookbook
A Witch's Beverages and Brews
The Witch's Book of Wisdom
paganwiccan.about.com/cs/kitchenwitch/
www.branwenscauldron.com/resources/kitchen.html
www.iit.edu/~phillips/personal/index.html
www.thymewise.net/kw/

MAHLORIAN GREEN CRAFT: A MYSTERY FAYERIE TRADITION
By Mahlora Christensen and Chuck Thelen

The Mahlorian Green Craft Tradition has no formal beginning and is never ending; it is always evolving and ever growing. The founders began working together approximately 10 years ago, and forming a particular Tradition was never our intent. Nonetheless, over time, we discovered that definite patterns and preferences had developed, and we realized the Goddess had guided us to the birthing of a new Tradition. While there are many ways to spell "fairy," we have chosen the spelling "fayerie," from archaic English. We found it blended the old language with the new Tradition, forming a bridge between old and new, and this spelling of the word also resonates in our magickal hearts.

Our system is one of active association with the Wild Natural World, and we are Wild Witches indeed. We perceive the Goddess as "the Green Goddess," or "Lady Green," the God as "the Green Man" or "Lord Green," with the Fayerie and Elementals being one and the same. All workings in the Mahlorian Tradition involve inclusion of the Lady Green and the Fayerie, with the Lord Green, when appropriate.

Our philosophy embraces living life to its fullest and in its most magickal form. Therefore, the core of our rituals and celebrations as well as our everyday lives are based heavily upon music, dance, poetry, and sensuality. It is our belief that we are here in this place and time to love and grow spiritually and to offer our guidance when it is so desired. We view energy as natural and pure, neither good nor bad, neither black nor white. It is only human perception and intent that denotes otherwise.

An Initiate in our Tradition is first and foremost a priestess/priest of the Goddess; any human hierarchy is secondary. We use the terms *High Priestess* and *High Priest*, but only to denote who is leading a particular ritual. For all other times and purposes, the members are equals. We do not initiate one to become a Witch, for that is between that person and Deity. We initiate one into our Tradition not by the passing of "power," but rather by the sharing and blending of natural energies, including our own as well as the Fayerie. The rule of study for a year and a day is a valid guideline but can vary, depending on ones experience and heartfelt knowledge.

Our standards of conduct boil down to "do no harm." Under no circumstance, other than self-defense or defense of loved ones, do we harm another. To do so would qualify one for immediate dismemberment (pun intended). If one truly follows this guideline, no further explanation is necessary.

The use of ritual tools is not prescribed by our Tradition; we leave that choice to the individual. Our moon circles are cast widdershins, and our Sabbat circles, deosil. If one does choose to wear clothing, it should be something that helps transform the mundane into the magickal.

> *Are we the Fay, this we cannot say*
> *Are we not the Fay, this we cannot say.*
> *Are we a kin to the Fay, yes to this we say.*

CONTACT

E-mail: mahloramoon@yahoo.com

FURTHER READING

We do not base this Tradition on "book learned" knowledge, however there are a few books that we have found helpful, as well as enjoyable, on our way.

All titles by Scott Cunningham

Drawing Down the Moon by Margot Adler

The Encyclopedia of Witches and Witchcraft by
    Rosemary Ellen Guiley

Green Witch Craft by Ann Moura
    A series of three books.

The Power of Myth by Joseph Campbell

The Spiral Dance by Starhawk

Stories of the Wild Spirit by Poppy Palin
    A book and tarot deck.

The Woman's Encyclopedia of Myths and Secrets by
    Barbra G. Walker

Wheel of the Year by Pauline Campanelli

www.witchvox.com/trads/trad_mgc.html

ABOUT THE CONTRIBUTOR

Mahlora is the Mother of Mahlorian Green Craft—a Mystery Fayerie Tradition—and is currently writing a book on the Tradition. She now resides in Tacoma, Washington, where, for the last 11 years, she has taught classes and workshops, led rituals, and participated in local Pagan events. She was involved in one of the first groups to hold public Pagan celebrations in this area and in leading the first local Witches Against Religious Discrimination (WARD) event. She is an ordained minister, through Spiritual Healers and Earth Stewards (SHES), and a Reiki Master, and she has led her current ring/coven for four years.

MI'NERWEN TRADITION
By Tra'nerDrakon

The Mi'nerwen Tradition is more than just a system of belief. Based on an organized Shamanic system, it is a complete culture with a rich history, mythology, and etiquette.

There has been some controversy surrounding the origins of the Mi'nerwen Tradition, because until recently, the Tradition was more or less a secret society. Like many other Pagan Traditions that survived the Dark Ages, the Mi'nerwen Tradition chose to hide from those who would destroy it, passing their knowledge down as an oral Tradition. It has only been over the past couple of years that they have chosen to risk becoming more public again, primarily because their dwindling numbers have forced them to either become more public or finally die out as a Tradition.

Mi'nerwen scholars are working hard to piece together archeological evidence that might shed some light on the verity of our legends. What we know for fairly certain is that the Order of Tra was one of the groups that Gerald

Gardner studied and based many of the ideas in his Tradition on. We also know that the founder of the Order of Tra was a woman named Tra'Kama, around whom many Mi'nerwen legends center. Her teachings, passed down via word of mouth, are the direct basis for the beliefs and teachings of the Order of Tra. A mytho-historical figure, Tra'Kama was a great leader who banded together a number of prehistoric tribes, bringing about a new society—one that was fairly advanced for its time. Few solid facts are known about the historical Tra'Kama, as we have only our legends to go by.

Today the Order of Tra and the followers of the Mi'nerwen Tradition in general are at the forefront of the growing Wiccan/Pagan Reform movement. The goal of the Reform is to preserve and, in some cases, completely resurrect some of the pre-Gardnerian Traditions that have suffered as a result of the growing popularity of newer, more popular Traditions. The Reform hopes to combat this by helping to make more in-depth material available to everyone, so that people can make more educated decisions about which Paths are truly for them.

The Mi'nerwen Tradition is very diverse, in the true Shamanic style. There is no worship, so to speak, of any one deity, or group of deities. Instead, individuals are encouraged to search out their own spirit guides and learn from them individually. There is some framework to the basic philosophy. The Order of Tra teaches that everything in the universe, indeed the universe itself, is all part of the Tree of Life. The Tree is a fractal ocean of probability. Every person chooses her own Path along the Tree's infinite branches. It is within this framework—the belief that we are all part of the universe and of each other—that the personal journey of every Mi'nerwen takes place.

Another important aspect of Mi'nerwen philosophy is honor. Mi'nerwens adhere to an unwritten code of honor

that directs them to always think for themselves, be pro-
ductive and contribute to society, love everyone, and be
creative and original. Laziness is considered about the most
dishonorable attribute of which a Mi'nerwen can be accused.

The Mi'nerwen Tradition is also very matriarchal.
Today men and women in the Mi'nerwen Tradition are
more or less equal, but some of the matriarchy still remains, as well as a fairly feminine perspective on the universe. This doesn't mean that men are unwelcome in the
Mi'nerwen Tradition; to the contrary, for the first time in
the history of the Order of Tra, men are being allowed to
join the Order. In fact, the current regent is male. (The
regent is administrating the Order until someone is ready
to take over as the *Penlunatra*.)

The Order branches out into eight disciplines, and each
member, while having a smattering of training in each of
the disciplines, specializes in one of the eight. The eight
disciplines are Culture, Philosophy, Physics, Healing, History, Language, Divination, and Art. The role of the Order of Tra in the Mi'nerwen Tradition is that of advisors
and teachers, as well as scientists, and skilled artisans. The
Order of Tra preserves and enhances the culture of the
Mi'nerwen Tradition, and training with the Order of Tra
is the primary method of secondary education for
Mi'nerwens pursuing the arts and sciences.

In terms of conduct, the Wiccan Rede is a good example of the basic philosophy Mi'nerwens take to life—
do what you want, so long as you do not harm or dishonor
those around you. In the event that disagreements arise,
one of the primary jobs of the head of each coven is to
arbitrate disputes among members of the coven. In
Mi'nerwen society, there were three honorable ways to
settle a dispute: negotiation, arbitration, or a duel. When
a disagreement was obviously not going to be solved on its
own, a Mi'nerwen would issue a challenge to another, who
would then choose between arbitration and a duel.

There is not a lot of "worship" in the Mi'nerwen Tradition. Mi'nerwen spirituality is based around mentoring. Mi'nerwens look for mentors among the spirit realm who can help guide them on their Path through the Tree of Life. These mentors take the form of spirit guides and ancestors. Mi'nerwens place a lot of value on receiving advice from one's ancestors. Instead of praying to one's ancestors for help, as many cultures do, Mi'nerwens most often implore their ancestors for inspiration to help them solve their own problems, and by doing so, bring their family honor. The idea of asking for someone to do something for you, instead of doing it yourself and taking responsibility for what you do, is not popular in Mi'nerwen culture. Honor is gained by taking responsibility, not by sloughing it off. As such, the Mi'nerwen dynamic of interaction with deities and spirits is entirely different from many other belief systems.

CONTACT

E-mail: tra_nerdrakon@orderoftra.org
   mydrin@orderoftra.org
   princess_athukama@orderoftra.org

FURTHER READING

"A Guide to the Mi'nerwen Tradition" by My'dRin
   (Available for free download at *www.speak-free.net/
   star-moon/orderoftra/modules.php?name=News&file
   =article&sid=9.*)
www.orderoftra.org/
   Order of Tra home page.
www.phoenician-alliance.org/
   Contains a lot of Mi'nerwen Tradition information.
www.witchvox.com/trads/trad_minerwen.html

ABOUT THE CONTRIBUTOR

Tra'nerDrakon was born Evelyn Kandratovich in Charleston, South Carolina, in the late 1970s. Having been raised primarily Catholic, she did not learn of the existence of Wicca and other Pagan Traditions until about the age of 13. After that, she worked hard to become involved in the Pagan community. A singer by trade, she changed her name to Tra'nerDrakon and was inducted into the Order of Tra's TrekLuna (Art and Music) Discipline, as a cleric, at the age of 16. Since then, she has been an active member of the Wiccan/Pagan reform community, and a strong supporter and promoter of the Order of Tra, and the Mi'nerwen culture. Recently, at the age of 24, she was ordained as a High Priestess of the Order of Tra's TrekLuna Discipline. Now, at nearly 30 years of age, Tra'nerDrakon sits on the Order of Tra Council of High Priests and Priestesses and works full time as an artist, singer, and clergywoman. She is also married to My'dRin, the acting regent of the Order of Tra, and has one daughter, born in 2002.

MINOAN TRADITION
By Sabazius, of StarDove Coven, With Assistance From Various Minoan Initiates and Elders

The Minoan Tradition began with the work of Eddie Buczynski, founder of the New York Welsh Tradition and the Wicca Tradition; Carol Bulzone, of Enchantments in New York; and Lady Rhea, of Magickal Realms in the Bronx. All three of the founding Minoan Elders were also Elders in various branches of Traditional Witchcraft who wanted a place of peace and celebration for Gay and Lesbian Witches. The Minoan Tradition has three branches represented in the Minoan Brotherhood, the Minoan Sisterhood, and the Cult of Rhea/Cult of the Double Axe.

The Minoan Brotherhood is a men's ritual Witchcraft Tradition founded in the mid-1970s by Eddie Buczynski, a Gardnerian and Welsh Elder and classical scholar. Its emphasis has always been on creating a safe and sacred place for gay and bisexual men to work Witchcraft, but we have never excluded heterosexual men who are comfortable working in our Way. The Minoan Sisterhood, founded at the same time in 1975, is a women's Tradition founded on Eddie's initial work by Lady Miw (Carol Bulzone) and Lady Rhea. The Sisterhood grew quickly from its founding, but seems to have largely remained a predominantly New York phenomenon.

The Cult of Rhea/Cult of the Double Axe represents the meeting ground between the Minoan Sisterhood and the Minoan Brotherhood. One must be a properly prepared Initiate of the Minoan Brotherhood or the Minoan Sisterhood in order to be part of the The Cult of Rhea/ Cult of the Double Axe, as it has no separate initiations or elevations of its own. It currently has no outer-court existence of its own, though some rudimentary materials that are shared among certain Brotherhood and Sisterhood groves have been written by Minos Sabazius of Toronto.

The Minoan Brotherhood and Sisterhood practice within a similar structure to most Traditional Witchcraft groups born out of the Gardnerian Diaspora. Minoan covens are overseen by a Third Degree Elder, also known as a *Minos* in the Brotherhood and *High Priestess* in the Sisterhood. Each Coven is autonomous and self-sustaining. Groves/covens tend to be secretive, non-proselytizing, and selectively careful about public involvement.

The core beliefs of the Minoan Tradition, in both the Brotherhood and Sisterhood, center around the worship of the ancient Cretan Snake Goddess, the Great Mother of the Aegean civilizations, and her divine son, the Starry Bull of the Heavens. Some Minoan Brotherhood Covens, placing an emphasis on the God, work with a mythic structure

centered around twin sons—the Star God and the Bull God—
and their mystical union beneath the Great Eye of the Mother.
Each coven is free to develop their own practices in addition
to the framework established by our core materials.

Minoan Initiates are, in most covens/groves, encouraged to develop a personal ethic based upon the Law of
the Goddess, "For Love is My Law, Unto All Beings."
The Wiccan Rede is *not* taught or ascribed to within the
Brotherhood as an absolute that must be adhered to, but
many Minoan Elders see it as good advice to measure one's
actions against. There is no one absolute code of conduct
which is common to the entire Tradition.

CONTACT

E-mail: MinoanSeekers-owner@yahoogroups.com
    StarDove_Coven@yahoo.ca

FURTHER READING

The following books are recommended reading from
Minos Sabazius, of StarDove Coven, and will provide some
insight into our background and our interests.

Blossom of Bone by Randy P. Conner
The Minoans: Bronze Age Life in Early Crete by
    Rodney Castleden
Never Again the Burning Times: Paganism Revisited by
    Loretta Orion
The Witchcraft Fact Book by Eddie Buczynski
www.witchvox.com/trads/trad_minoan.html

ABOUT THE CONTRIBUTOR

Micheal Sabazius, is a writer, editorial assistant, and
diviner, residing in Toronto, Ontario. He has been an Elder

of the Minoan Brotherhood since 1997 and has facilitated the initiations and elevations of more than 16 men into the Tradition, half of whom have founded their own groves and covens at various places in the United States and Canada. He has been previously published in *The Encyolpedia of Modern Witchcraft and Neo-Paganism*, edited by S. Rabinovitch and J. Lewis.

MIXED GENDER DIANIC WICCA
By H. Byron Ballard

I made my dedication as a Dianic priestess in the winter of 1975. Almost 30 years later, I light three candles on my altar most mornings, take deep breaths, and meditate on life lived in service to the Great Mother. I am now an ordained Dianic High Priestess and I live my life in the lap of the Goddess. To be Dianic is to be empowered by the Divine Feminine all around us. It is to know that time moves in a never-ending spiral of energy and love. It is seeing the Mother's face in the world all around us—in the elements of Gaia, the darkness of Hecate, and the wildness of Kali.

First and foremost, we envision the Earth, which birthed and nourishes us, as female. We revel in all aspects of life on the planet and feel unbounding joy in living a Pagan life. The Earth is our mother and sister but, perhaps more exactly, she is our Grandmother. Wise, ancient, full of deep mysteries, and ultimately unknowable. The Earth is a woman, and she is Goddess. We honor her as home and womb/matrix of all life. We also respect her as an immensely complex system that is constantly engaged in the dual act of creation and destruction. This is an awe-inspiring power with which we are suitably awed.

Structurally, Dianic Wicca is affirmingly nonhierarchical. Consensus-building is a conscious part of our decision-making and our spiritual practice. Magical workings are only undertaken with the unanimous consent of the workers. We meet in circles, groves, or covens, and our work is as inclusive of all present as possible. A High Priestess often functions as the ritualist of the group and as group mother.

You may be asking yourself how it's possible to have a mixed gender Dianic group. How is it that men can be called to delight in and worship the Divine Mother? Perhaps they've found a spiritual community that honors them as cocreators and gives them a nonthreatening environment in which they can explore their deeply loving natures. Maybe they have found a noncompetitive and nonhierarchical place where they can be awed by the destructive/creative nature of the universe and the mirror image of it in their own psyches, or they have found a place of deep personal connection with that which they deem Divine, and it is a healing and joyous homecoming. These are some of the things that drew me to a Dianic Path and I would be naive to think they would not draw others, regardless of gender.

Dianics perceive energy in different modalities. We find the ideas of "male and female energy" to be uncomfortable and limiting. Our concept of energy flows from the world around us—in the tides, the seasons, the jet stream. We perceive it in the Wheel of the Year, the Spiral, the triskele. It is an energy that surges and retreats, again and again. We see it in our human cycles of birth, growth, death, and rebirth. It is reflected in the phases of the moon and the silver wheel of the stars, in orgasm and the cycle of menstruation. We see few things as linear, preferring the wheel and spiral.

We expect a high standard of conduct from our Dianic sisters and brothers. We affirm that life, in all its mystery, is sacred; follow the Rede in all things; and try to be ever mindful of the Law of Return. We believe it is important to take responsibility for our actions as well as our reactions. Because it is difficult for us to separate our spiritual lives from our political ones, we are active in local politics, especially on any issue which affects freedom of religion as well as the environment. We believe that the Earth is all sacred space, and we refer to the cast Circle as *ritual* space, being mindful that every space is sacred.

We acknowledge that centuries of living under an autocratic and misogynistic culture has left gaping wounds in the human psyche. We accept that we must all be healers as well as ritualists and that we must salve spirits that are hurting and feed those that are hungry. We do this through ritual, as well as activism on behalf of oppressed people within our own communities.

To sum up the story of who we are and where we've been, we Dianics acknowledge a great debt to our ancient forebears; to those who lost their lives, properties, and will during the European Inquisitions; and to the people who kept alive a glowing ember of the Goddess through generations of Christian veneer. We thank those people who worshipped the Goddess in her aspect as Mary (along with all the "saints"), as well as those who kept their ancestral and household deities, passing them on (often in secret) to the next generation. We also thank the women and men in the early 1960s and 70s who gave the modern American Pagan movement its firm foundation, especially the MacFarlanes, Mary Daly, Starhawk, Z. Budapest, Marija Gimbutas, James Mellaart, and Sybil Leek.

CONTACT

E-mail: byronb@buncombe.main.nc.us

FURTHER READING

Ancient Mirrors of Womanhood by Merlin Stone
Cakes for the Queen of Heaven by Shirley Ann Ranck

Casting the Circle by Diane Stein
Descent to the Goddess by Sylvia Perera
A God Who Looks Like Me by Patricia Reilly
Goddesses and Gods of Old Europe by Marija Gimbutas
The Grandmother of Time by Z. Budapest
The Great Cosmic Mother by Monica Sjoo
The Great Mother and *Women of the Celts* by Jean Markale
Gyn-Ecology and *Beyond God the Father* by Mary Daly
The Holy Book of Women's Mysteries by Z. Budapest
Ladies of the Lake by Caitlin and John Matthews
The Once and Future Goddess by Elinor Gadon
The Return of the Mother by Andrew Harvey
The Serpent and the Goddess by Mary Condren
Shakti Woman by Vicki Noble
The Spiral Dance and *Dreaming the Dark* by Starhawk
www.witchvox.com/trads/trad_mgdianic.html

ABOUT THE CONTRIBUTOR

H. Byron Ballard is a Pagan advocate and writer living in the mountains of North Carolina.

MOHSIAN TRADITION
By Dana Corby, Senior High Priestess

The Mohsian Tradition of Wicca was founded in the early 1960s by Bill and Helen Mohs. It was not customary at that time for Craft groups to have names or consider themselves a "Tradition," but when it became necessary to call themselves something, they used American Eclectic Traditional Wicca (not related to the American Traditional Wicca based in Hawaii and best known as the home of Scott Cunningham). Within a few years of its inception, members and friends of Bill and Helen's group were calling it *Mohsian* and this is the name that stuck. Their home coven is known to have existed by 1965 and was eventually called *Pan's Garden*.

Mohsian is comprised of many threads from British Traditional and other sources. Much of our ritual is derived from early (pre-U.S.) Gardnerian and Alexandrian, with some of the loveliest passages from a British Celtic (Pagan, not Wiccan) Tradition called *Y Plant Bran*. Another interesting source is the Boread Tradition as transmitted by Thomas Giles, and there's even a snippet from New Reformed Orthodox Order of the Golden Dawn (NROOGD), used with permission. As with all older Books of Shadows, quite a lot of unattributed material, both published and unpublished, found its way in; we are currently engaged in research to find the sources of as much as possible and attribute it correctly. Mohsian is recognized as Brit-Trad by the New Wiccan Church International and is listed as such on the Beaufort House Website (see Further Reading).

Living the Witch's life was much more than just knowing and practicing a set of rituals—it was a matter of turning all you do into an expression of your Craft. The founders believed that it was important to know your local native plant and animal species, and nature hikes were a big part of coven life. Writing, art, music, gardening, even knowing how to make your own home repairs, all were seen as part of being a Witch. These teachings have become part of Mohsian lore.

The Mohsian Tradition still exists in essentially the same form as it did nearly 40 years ago. Self-reliance, creativity, study, and independent thinking are hallmarks of the Tradition. To an extent, so is cantankerousness. Mohsians work at keeping our feet on the ground. Most of us find being called *Lady* or *Lord* a bit too grand, and just go by our Craft names, sans title. Though all existing Mohsian covens derive from me, I style myself only Senior

High Priestess, not "Queen." I encourage whoever succeeds me to do likewise.

As an aside, the Mohsian Tradition that developed in Phoenix is quite different from the version I've passed on personally, reflecting its founders' interests in alchemy and Native American religion. By now, the Phoenix Branch differs enough from the rest of us that it's almost its own Tradition, yet their Coven of Danu is the oldest existing Mohsian coven. California Mohsian covens also have a very different flavor than my own and daughter covens.

In 1988, a radical and more ceremonious offshoot from Mohsian developed. Envisioned as an order of chivalry, as well as a priesthood, it honors both the Tuatha de Danaan and the Vanir. It subscribes to the belief (based on linguistic and other evidence) that the two pantheons are essentially the same, and in particular that Vana and Dana are the same primal Goddess. Titles of priests and priestesses are *Knight* and *Dame*.

Generally, however, as a British Tradition, Mohsian subscribes to belief in the Triple Goddess and the Dual God; most of us independently came to worship them under the same names, which we do not reveal to outsiders. We honor both ancestral and local spirits under many names and in many guises. We follow the Wheel of the Year. We possess the Ordains, cherish the Rede, and follow the Law of Threefold Return. As an older Tradition, however, we also say that, "No one keeps a Witch's conscience."

The connection to the local natural environment remains at the core of Mohsian. Most of us have a special closeness to our local tree species. In Phoenix, some of us are also drawn to the local stones. Wildcrafting and herbalism are seen as important, and a few are actively involved in tracing forgotten ley-lines.

The Mohsian Tradition is comprised of autonomous covens, each led by a High Priestess and High Priest. While we network among ourselves, there is no mechanism to enforce "orthodoxy" and no requirement for coven leaders to report upline. Practice and policy varies from coven to coven, but love of the Tradition seems to be pretty much universal, and people make an effort to preserve it.

Because of the traditional coven autonomy, Mohsians worship in many different ways. However there are some central similarities. Mohsians laugh a lot, hug a lot, and make a lot of truly dreadful puns. Some of our most successful spells and rituals over the years have been based on puns or jokes—whatever liberates the energy. A Mohsian ritual will be recognizable as British Traditional in origin, yet will have its own unique energy and rhythm, a poetry all its own.

CONTACT

E-mail: dana.corby@juno.com
Address: Mohsian Tradition
    c/o Tree House Productions
    6824 19th St. W, PMB 231
    University Place, WA 98466-5500

FURTHER READING

Drawing Down the Moon by Margot Adler
Keepers of the Flame, Interviews with Elders of Traditional Witchcraft in America by Morgana Davies and Aradia Lynch
www.geocities.com/SoHo/5756/tradlist.html
    Beaufort House Index of British Traditions.
www.newwiccanchurch.com/
    New Wiccan Church International.
www.witchvox.com/trads/trad_mohsian.html
    Full article.

ABOUT THE CONTRIBUTOR

Dana Corby is High Priestess in the Moon Tree Coven, a Senior High Priestess in the Mohsian Tradition of Wicca, founding priestess of the Wiccan Order of the Northern Lights, a bard in the Reformed Druids of North America, and fomer director of Tacoma Earth Religions Revival Association (TERRA).

NEW ENGLAND COVENS OF TRADITIONALIST WITCHES (NECTW)
By Rhiannon and Tuan Cu Mhara

The New England Covens of Traditionalist Witches (NECTW) was founded by Lady Gwen Thompson (1928–1986), a hereditary Witch from New Haven, Connecticut. It is with the utmost respect that the Elders of the NECTW dedicate this essay to the loving memory and the living Tradition of Gwen Thompson.

Gwen's impact on the development of the Craft today is undeniable. She is most widely known as the source of The Wiccan Rede. Most Witches are familiar with the Rede, yet its origin is often shrouded in confusion. The Wiccan Rede first appeared in print in 1975 in *Green Egg* magazine, in an article by Gwen Thompson titled "Wiccan-Pagan Potpourri." She attributed her Tradition's version of the Rede to her paternal grandmother, Adriana Porter, "who was well into her 90's when she crossed over into the Summerlands in 1946."

The simplistic nature of the Rede is due to the fact that many of the old ones were ordinary country people who received little or no formal education or were very simple in their ways. This included their rituals, practices, and wording. They were not taught to strive for perfection, but for wisdom. Because of the level of persecution at the time, they were unable to openly express themselves, so they resorted to symbolism in ritual, legend, and drawings, and preserved their sacred heritage in the most comprehensive manner. Here it is as it originally appeared in *Green Egg* (Vol. viii, No. 69):

REDE OF THE WICCAE
(THE COUNSEL OF THE WISE ONES)

1. Bide the Wiccan laws ye must in perfect love and perfect trust

2. Live and let live—fairly take an fairly give

3. Cast the Circle thrice about to keep all evil spirits out

4. To bind the spell every time, let the spell be spake in rhyme

5. Soft of eye and light of touch—speak little, listen much

6. Deosil go by the waxing Moon—sing and dance the Wiccan rune

7. Widdershins go when the Moon doth wane, an the Werewolf howls by the dred Wolfsbane

8. When the Lady's Moon is new, kiss the hand to her times two

9. When the Moon rides at her peak, then your heart's desire seek

10. Heed the Northwind's mighty gale—lock the door and drop the sail

11. When the wind comes from the South, love will kiss thee on the mouth

12. When the wind blows from the East, expect the new and set the feast

13. When the West wind blows o'er thee, departed spirits restless be

14. Nine woods in the Cauldron go—burn them quick an burn them slow

15. Elder be ye Lady's tree—burn it not or cursed ye'll be

16. When the Wheel begins to turn—let the Beltane fires burn

17. When the Wheel has turned a Yule, light the Log an let Pan rule

18. Heed ye flower, bush an tree—by the Lady blessed be

19. Where the rippling waters go, cast a stone an truth ye'll know

20. When ye have need, hearken not to other's greed

21. With the fool no season spend or be counted as his friend

22. Merry meet an merry part—bright the cheeks an warm the heart

23. Mind the Threefold Law ye should—three times bad an three times good

24. When misfortune is enow, wear the blue star on thy brow

25. True in love ever be unless thy lover's false to thee

26. Eight words the Wiccan Rede fulfill—an it harm none, do what ye will

It is important to note that the spiritual significance, tenets, and principles contained within the Rede are explained fully to the initiated Witch and remain an oathbound teaching. Much of our lore, including much of the Rede's significance, is transmitted orally. Gwen's family Tradition was handed down through many generations and blended with popular occultism to the present form she named NECTW. Not all who are born into a family Tradition are destined to follow this Path, and Gwen feared her Tradition would die out and fade into obscurity. This was the principal reason she decided to "foster" individuals outside her blood family in order to ensure that the Tradition would survive.

Today, NECTW is a place for men and women to be trained as priests and priestesses of the Craft. The teachings and intense training are not for everyone. They require a strong follower with a particular sense of dedication and a sincere heart, willing to train and practice in order to understand the ways of the Wise. Those seeking to join this Tradition are ideally of keen mind, strong spirit, and able body and are ready to study the Old Ways and make this Path an integral part of their life. NECTW Initiates are interested in folklore; meditation; ritual concepts; Celtic history; literature; philosophy; music and art; ecology; herbal lore; runecraft; spellcraft; astrology; tarot; and divination by crystal, pendulum, and board. We do not charge any fees, but all are expected to contribute their share to circles and feasts.

The Book of Shadows is always copied by hand and each degree of elevation must be mastered fully before elevation. We are quite informal, and a key word in our Tradition is *family*. Unity, harmony, courtesy, respect, study, devotion, and dedication to the gods and each other are greatly emphasized. Circles are held outdoors at night, unless the weather brings them inside.

Within the umbrella of NECTW are several branches, including Tuatha de Danann Tradition (TDD) and the Welsh Rite Gwyddonaid. Outside of the Tradition, Gwen Thompson's teachings have led to the founding of and have

influenced many Craft Traditions in the United States—
some of which are still active today, including New York
Welsh Tradition, Blue Star Tradition (via New York Welsh
Tradition), Georgian Tradition, Keepers of the Ancient
Mysteries (KAM), and the StarBorne Tradition. She was
an influence on many Gardnerian and Alexandrian Elders
as well.

CONTACT

Website: *www.NECTW.org*
> Contains information about Gwen Thompson and
> the NECTW, with a link to e-mail any questions
> regarding Gwen or the NECTW.

E-mail: Rhiannon@cox.net

ABOUT THE CONTRIBUTORS

Rhiannon and Tuan Cu Mhara work in the main offices of the NECTW and have been practicing members
for many years.

NEW YORK WELSH TRADITION
By Tuan Cú Mhara, High Priest and Elder

New York Welsh Traditionalists are first and foremost
followers of the Old Gods—the Great Moon Goddess of
Rebirth and her consort, the Horned God of Hunting,
Death, and Magic. In this regard, the NY Welsh Tradition
is no different than any other branch of Witchcraft practiced in America today.

However, the majority of this Tradition was written
by its founder, Edmund M. Buczynski, also known as Lord
Gwydion or Lord Hermes (depending on the year), and is

a true testament to his poetic brilliance and insight. There were also contributions from Leo Louis Martello (Lord Lupus/Nemesis), who wrote part of the Third Degree (according to Leo anyway), and Lord Gwydion acquired pieces of Gardnerian rituals through various sources, including Herman Slater (Lord Govannan) of the Warlock Shoppe—a notorious occult shop in Brooklyn in the early to mid-1970s.

It was out of the Warlock Shoppe that Lord Gwydion founded the Brooklyn Heights Coven with Kay Smith (Lady Melusine) on October 21, 1972. Lord Gwydion also received some material from his first initiating High Priestess, Lady Gwen Thompson (founder of the New England Covens of Traditionalist Witches, or NECTW), but this was not enough material to be relevant, and the NECTW is not associated or affiliated with the late Edmund M. Buczynski or the NY Welsh Tradition.

Lord Gwydion was a prolific writer but never satisfied, and he was constantly changing and adding to his personal Book of Shadows. Because of this, his Initiates throughout the NY Welsh Tradition had variations of the NY Welsh Tradition Book of Shadows, depending upon when they were initiated—including his Priestess, Lady Melusine (aka Lady Vivienne or Lady Goewin, depending on the year). Ed Buczynski was so inspired by the Old Ones that he also created the Wica Tradition (a neo-Gardnerian Tradition), and the Minoan Brotherhood (a Craft Tradition for homosexual men).

Within the NY Welsh Tradition, rituals are always worked male to female, in accordance with the natural balance between the Goddess and Horned God. The Tradition does not, however, discriminate against those of other sexual preference, as long as those people are well adjusted in themselves and can work heterosexually within the circle.

This Tradition's version of the Great Rite, which is an essential part of many Craft Traditions (including the Gardnerian and Alexandrian Traditions of Wicca), is performed only in token, unless in private by those bound in love. In this age, a fertility of the mind tends to be stressed more than of the body. Within the covens, it is the High Priestess who leads most of the rituals, with the High Priest as her assistant. The High Priestess is also the "supreme authority" within the coven, advised by her High Priest and any of the Third Degree within the coven. However, it is recognized that the influence of the High Priest is greater during the cold months of the year when the power of the Great Horned God is considered to be stronger, because the High Priest is his representative made manifest on the physical plane.

This Tradition also works robed, and dance and chants are an integral part of the NY Welsh Tradition ritual. The 13 Esbats, eight Sabbats, plus the Festival of Lights and Elder Circles are a time of deep religious experience with the Old Ones and fellow coveners, as well as a time of joyous dance, laughter, wit, and wine. Only a very few covens have emerged from hiding, as this Tradition is historically an underground one, in accordance with the "Old Laws." The reason for this is simple enough: they do not wish their rites and mysteries to be used or abused by those not properly prepared through initiation and elevation, or stolen for personal gain and glorification/legitimization— something which is happening of late with ever increasing vigor, as the "Witch craze" becomes more popular, and people not qualified to lead others become desperate for validation or material.

Lord Gwydion regarded the gods as symbolic of the forces in nature, and strived to work in harmony with them. He believed we should never do anything to work against nature in any way, as he believed that whatever we do, for good or evil, must return unto us threefold. This is known as the Rule of Three. In this regard, he believed the forces of nature and the universe *may* be used for good or evil, but it is purely up to the individual who must consider the issue and accept the consequences of their actions. Because we are aware all is returned threefold, we as a Tradition prefer not to cause any harm, unless it is in self-defense—which is entirely permissible according to the universal law of self-preservation.

The New York Welsh Tradition is very concerned with maintaining the harmony of the environment and seeks to preserve the beauty of the Earth and the life of all its creatures. Likewise, the members of this Tradition strive for balance within in order and to be one with all things.

CONTACT

E-mail: Gwyddonaid@cox.net

ABOUT THE CONTRIBUTOR

Lord Tuan Cú Mhara was initiated into the New York Welsh Tradition in the early 1980s. He was High Priest of the Cauldron of Cerridwen Coven in New York City and remains an Elder of the Tradition today.

OAK AND STONE PATH
By Lady Willow

Founded in 2000 by Lady Willow, Lady Zabella, Lord Oak, Trinity Rhiannon, and Clarity, Oak and Stone Path has evolved over the years. In 1999 I received my ordination as an interfaith minister. Shortly thereafter, a group of people from various spiritual backgrounds and I formed an interfaith church called Gateway to the Sacred-Interfaith Fellowship. This group met for two years before small subgroups began to form within the larger congregation. One such group emerged as a coven—The Coven of the Sacred Stone People. The founding members of this Coven came from backgrounds in Eclectic-Celtic Wicca, Shamanism, and Druidry. A blending of the knowledge and experience of the founding members, along with a lot of experimentation, has given birth to the Oak and Stone Path.

Ethically, we follow closely to Universal Life Church standards. With regard to deity, each member honors the Lord and Lady in their own way. Many pantheons are called upon. Some of us work closely with a certain God or God-dess, but as a group, no particular deity or deities are defined as being "Oak and Stone Path" deities.

Our garb is somewhat unique to us. We have tunics with the coven logo on the front, which we wear over our robes. Our young maidens and lads wear blue robes, our older maidens white, mothers red, crones black, and priests white or green. Beyond this, our tools include an altar box, which bears our candles, incense, and other necessary items.

We are privileged to have a lovely 400-acre sanctuary to call our covenstead, as of 2001. We have constructed a permanent stone circle along side the creek that runs through the property. Beneath a ring of oaks, this circle is our primary place of worship and celebration. We also have two other dedicated circles that we use from time to time.

We hold two open festivals each year, at Beltane and Samhain. The Sanctuary is also available for camping, hiking, retreats, special events, rites of passagem and so on. Following is a sample from our circles, a full moon poem read during ritual.

Full Moon Poem

Ritual time has come at last.

There is no future, there is no past.

A time out of time, a place out of place,

We cleanse and consecrate this sacred space.

Call the Elements one by one,

For the Circle is cast, and our work has begun.

The East, the Air, the Wand, the Wind,

Communication, thought, and creativity send.

The South, the Fire, the Sword, the Flame,

Passion, drive, and ambition we claim.

The West, the Water, the Cup, the Wave,

Bring us the emotion, love,
and empathy we crave.

The North, the Earth, the Stone, the Salt,

May we be grounded, steady,
dependable, to a fault.

Our Lord, our Lady, lend us your ear:

Your wisdom, caring, and power draw near.

May the work now begin as we have prepared,

Results shall be threefold
and the bounty be shared.

CONTACT

Website: *www.sacredaoks.org*

E-mail: willowwitch@yahoo.com (Lady Willow)
    LadyZabella@yahoo.com (Lady Zabella)

Address: Sacred Oak Sanctuary
    P.O. Box 769
    Pearce, AZ 85625

OPHIDIAN TRADITIONAL WITCHCRAFT
By Tony Steele

The Ophidian or Serpent-venerating Traditional Craft has been around for a very long time. One of its magical texts, the *Oera Linda Book*, has sections that date back more than 4,000 years. Every ancient culture recognized a primordial Serpent-deity associated with wisdom and power, dwelling in the watery abyss deep below the Earth's surface. In more recent centuries, this ancient belief was kept alive by traveling folk, especially those who lived and worked on the sea, on rivers, and (later) on canals. Knowledge of the World Serpent also persisted in remote country districts all over Europe.

The *Oera Linda Book* was compiled over many centuries by the Frisians who, in historical times, lived around the southern coast of the North Sea. The Frisians believed that their ancestors had constructed the stone circles and megalithic monuments that are found all over Europe. They also claimed to be descended from the inhabitants of the lost island of Atlantis (or *Atland*, as they called it). The ancient Megalithic Culture existed across the whole of western and northern Europe, and was the earliest known civilization on Earth. The Greek philosopher Plato and the *Oera Linda Book* both tell us that this vast area was divided into 10 autonomous kingdoms, or kin-groups, spread out over large tracts of the continent.

The remains of the Megalithic Culture can be seen to this day in the form of cromlechs, dolmens, barrows, and stone circles such as Stonehenge. The earliest of these crypts, or temples, have been dated to around 4800 BC, so this gives us a reasonable starting point for the long and convoluted history of the Ophidian Craft—though some would say that it is as old as the human race itself.

Today, the Ophidian Traditional Craft is preserved and passed on by the Ordo Anno Mundi (OAM), which has branches in both Europe and North America. Based in Staffordshire, England, the OAM was founded on March 18, 1985, and traces its initiatory lineage to the Frisian-descended canal folk of the English Midlands. This illustrious lineage is passed on to all of its Initiates who undergo the training.

The two words that best sum up the Ophidian view of reality are *animism* and *polytheism*. Literally everything is alive, with its own sentience and feelings. Nature abounds with spirits of every kind, many of which are powerful enough to be classed as deities, either gods or goddesses (or sometimes androgynous).

Ophidians see all gods and goddesses as individuals, and do not conflate them all together as "aspects" of each other. They venerate Mother Earth (called *Irtha* in the *Oera Linda Book*) as the most powerful of the goddesses, mother of all the others. They also, of course, venerate the World Serpent, *Wr-alda*, who fertilizes Mother Earth with his life force. Together the World Serpent and Mother Earth brought forth three daughters (Lyda, Finda, and Frya), the mothers of the human race. In addition, there is the Horned God (Fosite, or Wodin), who is seen as the messenger of the World Serpent.

Water is the physical manifestation of the World Serpent and is therefore seen as the most magical of Elements. In vast oceans, wide rivers, and tiny streams, it moves in sinuous, serpentine motions across the Earth, bringing life to everything it touches. Flowing water is always accompanied by whorls and spirals of telluric energy—the invisible force that sustains all living things, including deities and spirits.

Ophidians also lay great emphasis on the veneration of ancestors. Indeed, many of their rituals involve the summoning of their ancestors to physical manifestation. The shades of the dead survive by regular infusions of the life-force from those still living, and mostly dwell in one of the Seven Hells that make up the Underworld. In a sense, their nature is vampiric (a word which has suffered much distortion in popular culture). Yet at the same time, most Ophidians accept a form of reincarnation—though the specific ideas about this may vary slightly among individuals.

Like most branches of the Traditional Craft, Ophidian Witchcraft is primarily organized into orders (sometimes called *clans*). Not all members of an order will be Initiates, however—some will be Neophytes awaiting initiation, and others, for example, will be family members who have no particular desire to undergo the training. Until the 1940s, the Ophidian Craft was very much family-based.

Some orders have six initiatory degrees, and others, such as the OAM, have seven. One has abolished degrees altogether. These changes have come about through natural evolution within each order, as indeed have all the other differences. Typically, there will be an Outer Mysteries comprising the first three degrees, followed by an Inner Mysteries. Initiation into an order will usually be conducted when the candidate is alone—such is the case with the OAM. The initiation itself will involve some sort of physical or mental endurance. The new Initiate will then be plunged straight into an intensive training program.

The OAM uses a lunar calendar known as the *Kroder* to determine the dates of new and full moons. Covens tend to meet together for ritual purposes once a month, at new moon. There are also three traditional festival dates, derived from medieval practice, which are determined by the secular calendar—Old St Thomas's (January 1), Old St George's (May 4), and Old St Bartholomew's (September 4). Nowadays it is just as common for Ophidians to use the standard eight festivals of modern Paganism.

Ethically, we remain aware that all things in the universe—past, present, and future—are interconnected in a vast web of relationships. Everything we do affects everything else, mostly in ways that we cannot hope to understand. For this reason we should always be aware that any action or thought might have consequences far beyond its immediate objective. Yet the Ophidian Craft does not accept an immutable threefold (or indeed any other "-fold") law of return—the universe is far too subtle for that, and any specific numerical value we might like to place on such things is bound to be arbitrary.

Magic itself is a neutral force, like electricity or magnetism, and can be used for any purpose whatsoever. This must not be interpreted as a "Do whatever you want!" system. Experience teaches us that negativity breeds more negativity, so is best avoided. The fact is that those who are seriously committed to treading the magical Path will always develop a powerful set of personal morals and ethics. The point is that these are their own, not imposed by somebody else.

The OAM takes a very dim view of any member who brings the Craft into disrepute, either by abusing their position, or using magic for immoral purposes. Such people will be expelled.

The basic purpose of magic is to invoke or create non-physical entities, which are then given a specific function or task to perform—this is what we call a spell. The beings that are invoked have many designations, such as deities, spirits, thought-forms, and numerous others. In the Ophidian system no proper spell could be cast without invoking or creating (birthing) a non-corporeal entity to carry it out. Because the ability to invoke entities is fundamental to the practice of Traditional Witchcraft, all of the coven meetings are geared to this end. Ophidians will invoke or create any entity they deem proper to the occasion. Very often they will choose a being from their rich and diverse Elf-lore. Nature Spirits abound everywhere, living on land and in water. Rituals always take place outdoors, at night, usually around the time of the new moon.

CONTACT

Website: *www.angelfire.com/realm/oam*

E-mail: oamchief@yahoo.co.uk (in the United Kingdom)
    Raven7866@aol.com (in the United States)

Address: Coven of Cythrawl
    Orchard PO Box 0634
    Singapore 912322

FURTHER READING

Dragons of the West by Nigel Pennick

Oera Linda Book
    View full text online at *www.angelfire.com/realm/
    oam/oera.htm*

Rites and Rituals of Traditional Witchcraft by Tony
    Steele

Water Witches by Tony Steele

www.witchvox.com/trads/trad_ophidian.html

ABOUT THE CONTRIBUTOR

In 1985, Tony Steele founded the Ordo Anno Mundi (OAM), a magical order of Initiates dedicated to the training of its members in the arcane sciences of nature. His books include *Water Witches* and *Rites and Rituals of Traditional Witchcraft*, both published by Capall Bann.

RAVENMYST CIRCLE
By LadyHawke, the Mythmaker

At Yule 2001, four Elders and one Third Degree High Priestess were called to serve the community in a very different way. They collectively made the decision to forge a new Path for themselves, their respective covens, and their students. Thus RavenMyst Circle was born.

"Raven" is a totem honored by each of the founding covens, including our largest one. And "Myst" is for the mysteries we would be exploring, the mists that separate the mundane world from the spiritual one, the mists and fog that are "in between" places (being in between air and water and, therefore, places of great power), and the mystics of the ages, whose wisdom we embrace.

We have numerous Elders and teachers who have helped us in getting to where we are today. Among them, notable names include Gerald Gardener, Raymond Buckland, Michael Ragan, Lord Serphant, Lady Branwen, Lady Silver RavenWolf, and Lady Breid Foxsong. All five of RavenMyst's founders had already received their Third Degrees from Lady Silver RavenWolf before leaving Black Forest to found RavenMyst Circle.

In RavenMyst, we recognize that every Witch, regardless of age, sex, or rank is a thriving individual and that all are equal in the eyes of the gods. Our gods are those who came before mankind got around to naming them. In the oldest written language, the Goddess of Earth was called simply *Ki*, which was the Sumerian word for *Earth*. The Sky God was *An*, the word for *Heaven*. We call on the Lady of the Oceans, the Goddess of the Moon, Mother Earth. We call on the Lord of the Woodlands, the God of the Sun, Father Sky. If pressed to describe her, we might fall back on Oberon Zell's "Millennial Gaia," with DNA strands twining through her hair and all the living things of the universe sprouting upon her body. For him, we might turn to the mythical half-stag, half-man known as Pan or Herne, playing his magickal pipes, which mimics the breath of life throughout the forest. Each individual RavenMyst Witch identifies with her or his own ideals and has his or her own patron and matron deities. We recognize the gods both as real individuals, and as parts of a greater whole—just as we are each real individuals and yet parts of a greater whole.

RavenMyst is a five-tier Tradition consisting of Dedicant, First Degree, Second Degree, Third Degree, and Elder levels. All members enter at the Dedicant level. When they finish the level-one lessons, plus a year and a day of training, and/or when their teacher feels they are ready, they will be initiated to the First Degree. Initiates may elect to remain at First, or continue their work and training up through Second and Third Degree. Thirds who elect to take our counseling lessons—a curriculum created for us by Judy Harrow—will be given legal clergy status. Legal clergy will be able to sign documents pertaining to births, marriages, and passing, in accordance with laws in their state. In addition, all Third Degree members may form covens of their own.

Newcomers go through a careful screening process as we determine whether they will be a good fit with the group mind. As a rule, a newcomer will attend several coven gatherings and/or open circles before being invited to dedicate to one of our covens. Dedications and all elevations must be performed in person, even in the Cyber Coven. Long distance students have a much more difficult challenge than local ones, and while it's not fair, it is necessary. We are open to new seekers, though we do want them to be aware that we have an extremely limited number of teachers and, currently, only one Cyber Coven.

RavenMyst is incorporated as a Michigan nonprofit organization, and is in the process of applying for federal tax exemption. Thus, RavenMyst was created with a Guardian Council made up of the five founders plus two appointees, but with a plan in place to hold annual elections so that the seats of authority could rotate among the membership. Anyone of First Degree or higher may hold office and vote in the elections. The Guardian Council ensures fair policy-making and just governance of the group.

CONTACT

Website: *www.ravenmyst.org*
E-mail: WitchLadyHawke@aol.com

FURTHER READING

www.witchvox.com/trads/trad_ravenmystcircle.html

ABOUT THE CONTRIBUTOR

LadyHawke, the Mythmaker is otherwise known as *New York Times* best-selling novelist Maggie Shayne. A voracious researcher, she practiced and studied alone for nearly a decade before dedicating to the Black Forest Clan and Seminary where she began her formal training. She worked through the entire Black Forest Seminary's course of study, completing it in three years as she was elevated through the three degrees of Traditional Wicca.

She was a Third Degree High Priestess when she was called, along with a small group of Craft Elders, to forge a new Path. These five, along with their students and covens, came together to create RavenMyst Circle. LadyHawke is one of RavenMyst's five founders, and has personally authored many of the Tradition's rituals, along with much of the student curriculum. LadyHawke was Eldered in 2002. She is legal clergy, and sits on the board of directors (or "Guardian Council") of RavenMyst. She has served as Guardian Director since RavenMyst's inception at Yule 2001.

In addition, LadyHawke teaches a four-week Wicca 101 class at her local adult education center. She has taught Wicca 101 seminars for writers at numerous writers' conventions, conferences, and workshops and sat on a panel discussing Pagan Traditions at Cornell University in the fall of 2004. She owns and operates several Wiccan e-mail lists, in service to her community.

RECLAIMING TRADITION WITCHCRAFT
By M. Macha NightMare,
With Input From Vibra Willow

A note from Trish: *Starhawk's works were among the first I read as a young seeker (and I suspect I'm in good company).* The Spiral Dance *gave me foundations from which to build my Path.*

The Reclaiming Tradition of contemporary American Witchcraft arose from a working collective in the San Francisco Bay Area of California. In the Summer of 1980, Diane Baker and Starhawk—who had been working with individual guests to their coven, Raving, prior to that time—decided to plan and co-teach a basic class in Witchcraft (especially since Starhawk's book *The Spiral Dance* was due to be published later that year). It was a six-week series, and it was offered as a class in Goddess spirituality, directed towards women. Classes were done within sacred space and the emphasis was on the experiential rather than the didactic. In addition, each class demonstrated a different aspect of magic (the intellectual, energy sensing and projecting, trance work, spell-working, and so on) and built upon the preceding class.

This class was so enthusiastically received by the women who took it that they pleaded for more. From there, more classes were formed, more people began teaching, and more covens arose. This core group became the Reclaiming Collective, so naming itself in 1980.

Because of the political experiences of most of the early organizers of Reclaiming, the Collective has always used consensus process, learned mainly from the Religious Society of Friends (Quakers). This takes longer than traditional group decision-making and can be fraught with frustrations, especially for the more hierarchical and parliamentary-minded. Yet within Reclaiming, it fostered close bonds among participants.

This collective shared this statement early in its history: Reclaiming is a community of San Francisco Bay Area women and men working to unify spirit and politics. Our vision is rooted in the religion and magic of the Goddess—the Immanent Life Force. We see our work as teaching and making magic—the art of empowering ourselves and each other. In our classes, workshops, and public rituals, we train our voices, bodies, energy, intuition, and minds. We use the skills we learn to deepen our strength both as individuals and as a community, to voice our concerns about the world in which we live, and to bring to birth a vision of a new culture. Thus, unlike most other Craft Traditions, Reclaiming has always espoused a connection between spirituality and political action.

In 1985, we began offering intensives that later became known as "Witch Camps" and expanded with San Francisco Bay Area teachers being invited to other states, Canada, England, Germany, and Norway. Today, Reclaiming Tradition Witch Camps throughout the United States, Canada, and Europe are run autonomously.

In *The Pagan Book of Living and Dying*, Starhawk describes Reclaiming's style of ritual as EIEIO—Ecstatic, Improvisational, Ensemble, Inspired, and Organic—and explains that our practices are constantly growing, being "extended, refined, renewed and changed as the spirit moves us and need arises, rather than...learned and repeated in a formulaic manner."

Distinguishing features of Reclaiming Tradition Witchcraft are:

1. Nonhierarchical covens and group priesthoods or priestesshoods.

2. No specific pantheon and no requirement of initiation. When initiations are undertaken, they are customized.

3. Strong emphasis on political involvement and social and ecological responsibility and consciousness.

4. No set liturgy (except in certain large, rehearsed or semi-rehearsed public Sabbat rituals) but rather training in principles of magic and the structure of ritual, and how to "speak as the spirit moves you" within that structure.

5. Cultivation of ecstatic states (customarily without the use of entheogens or psychotropics) and divine colloquy—more Shamanic than ceremonial.

6. Cultivation of self-empowerment, creativity, and self-discovery.

7. Extensive use of chanting and breathwork in magical rites.

8. Intense energy-raising, often using our trademark spiral dance (or even double helix/DNA molecule dance).

9. Magical use of the Pentacle of Iron construct and its obverse, the Pentacle of Pearl.

10. Concept of Three Souls.

11. Encouragement of the creation of new ritual forms by anyone.

There is no doubt that Starhawk is the primary theologian of Reclaiming Tradition Witchcraft, as well as being its most prolific liturgist. Other prominent liturgists include Rose May Dance, Pandora Minerva O'Mallory, Anne Hill, T. Thorn Coyle, and the many collaborative chants and songs that arise from classes and in the various Witch Camps. People often assume Starhawk is the leader, but that has never been true, although she has always been and remains a powerful and influential voice.

Reclaiming Collective incorporated as a nonprofit religious corporation in the state of California in 1990, wrote bylaws based on a consensus process model of decision-making, and eventually gained 501(c)3 tax status with the U.S. Internal Revenue Service.

Realizing that we have no way, need or desire to dictate to others how they should perform their rituals and that we abhor dogma and stagnation, we believe that any Witch may honestly and sincerely claim to be a Reclaiming Tradition Witch if he or she practices Reclaiming-style magic and agrees to our Principles of Unity.

The values of the Reclaiming Tradition stem from our understanding that the Earth is alive and all of life is sacred and interconnected. Each of us embodies the Divine. Our ultimate spiritual authority is within, and we need no other person to interpret the sacred to us. We foster the questioning attitude and honor intellectual, spiritual, and creative freedom.

To us, all living beings are worthy of respect. All are supported by the sacred Elements of Air, Fire, Water, and Earth. We work to create and sustain communities and cultures that embody our values, that can help to heal the wounds of the Earth and her peoples, and that can sustain us and nurture future generations.

CONTACT

Website: *www.reclaiming.org*
E-mail: herself@machanightmare.com

FURTHER READING

www.starhawk.org/
www.machanightmare.com/

ABOUT THE CONTRIBUTOR

M. Macha NightMare has long been active in the Reclaiming Collective in the San Francisco Bay Area, is cocreator (with Starhawk) of *The Pagan Book of Living and Dying,* and author of *Witchcraft and the Web: Weaving Pagan Traditions Online* (November 2001 from ECW Press). She has been active in the Covenant of the Goddess (CoG) at all levels since 1981, and is a ritualist and presenter at festivals, stores, colleges, and radio and TV stations throughout the United States. Her work has appeared in *Reclaiming Quarterly*, *PanGaia*, *Green Egg*, *The Pomegranate*, *Hole in the Stone*, and other publications. For more information, refer to her Website, *www.machanightmare.com* and the Cherry Hill Seminary, where she chairs the public ministry department *www.cherryhillseminary.org*.

ROEBUCK TRADITION
By Ann and Dave Finnin

The Roebuck Tradition, as practiced by the Ancient Keltic Church, is a religious organization dedicated to the rediscovery and revival of the Pagan Mystery Faith of the ancient Celtic peoples, and the incorporation of this ancient faith into modern 20th-century America. It was founded in 1976 by Ann and David Finnin as an experimental group called The Roebuck, which was made up of members of many different magical systems devoted to the exploration of a British Mystery Tradition made public in Britain during the 1950s and introduced into the United States between 1964 and 1966 through the writings of Robert Cochrane.

Cochrane died in 1966. However, with the aid of the Cochrane writings and material contributed by other British traditionalists, the members of The Roebuck attempted to recreate this Tradition and, through trial and error, forged a Mystery School designed to teach its students the various methods of personal magical development.

In 1989, The Roebuck incorporated and became the Ancient Keltic Church, with all the rights and responsibilities pertaining to our legal status. Since then, we have worked to establish the Ancient Keltic Church as a modern-day Celtic Mystery School of the sort that might have come down to us from ancient times, had nearly 2,000 years of Christianity not intervened.

Philosophically, we carry on a Tradition that practices magic and taps into ancient and primal sources for the power to do so. We invoke the aid of unseen forces and use natural materials, such as stones, herbs, animals, and so forth, to channel our will in order to make things happen. But we are, above all, a Pagan religion with a complex theology and strict code of behavior. We believe that spiritual development comes first and that magic is secondary, coming once a certain level of attainment has been achieved. "Our belief," as Cochrane wrote in 1966, "is concerned with wisdom; our true name, then, is the Wise people and wisdom is our aim."

One of the ways in which this is accomplished is through contact with the inner plane guardians of the circle. These guardians, called gods and goddesses or "shining ones," are described in Irish, Welsh, and Gaelic folklore and are associated with the four Elements of Fire, Earth, Air, and Water. These guardians, along with a Father God and Mother Goddess, make up the pantheon of deities that are called upon to aid in any magical work that is done by the group to which a member is introduced, first through guided meditations and then through personal contacts. They include Bride, Lugh, Niahm, Cernnunos, Cerridwen, Nodens, Morrigan, and the Black Goddess, among others.

The Ancient Keltic Church has an Initiate priesthood which teaches students and runs circles. Membership in this priesthood requires a great deal of time, effort, and dedication and is not for everyone. Candidates are chosen with considerable care and many factors—particularly their sincerity and desire to work and study—are taken into account. The training can take as much as two years and requires a great deal of time and effort on the part of both student and teacher.

Initiation into the Roebuck Tradition, provided it is administered under the auspices of the Ancient Keltic Church, constitutes official ordination. The Initiate priest or priestess has the legal right to perform marriages, funerals, and other rites of passage in the community and also has access to hospitals, prisons, and other government offices as much as a member of any official clergy. Roebuck Initiates are also expected to be self-supporting members of the community and to abide by all local, state, and federal laws. Because the Roebuck is also a legal church, its members need to be mindful that their behavior can have a serious impact on the entire organization as a whole.

The key to the ethical code of the Roebuck Tradition is self-responsibility for all thoughts, words, and deeds, both in this world and in the magical realm. Personal honor, integrity, honesty, loyalty, and devotion to the gods, ancestors, and clan are ideals to be constantly pursued. We acknowledge that whatever we do to others—whether prompted by love or malice—rebounds back upon ourselves eventually, as the Dark Goddess constantly grinds the mill of fate and we reap what we have sown. However, with self-responsibility comes the necessity of making choices in the world. If we made no choices for ourselves, others would make choices for us, leading to passivity and victimhood—the direct antithesis to magical empowerment. We realize that choices are never cut and dried, and that often trade-offs have to be made. We must make the best choice we can in a given situation and then accept the consequences—both good and bad—of that choice.

The Roebuck Tradition shares most of the same Pagan holidays and festivals celebrated by most Neo-Pagan groups. These include the Celtic Fire Festivals of Samhain, Imbolc, Beltaine, Lughnasadh, and to a lesser extent, the solstices and equinoxes. We also celebrate the full moons and the dark moons. Often, a major festival is a time when all the daughter covens can circle together, reserving full and dark moons for individual coven work.

CONTACT

E-mail: Akcroebuck@aol.com

FURTHER READING

Lights from the Shadows by Gwyn
The first book which reveals many of the inner workings of the family Traditions.

The Rebirth of Witchcraft by Doreen Valiente
The late Doreen Valiente played an important part in the development both of the Gardnerian Tradition and the Clan of Tubal Cain.

The Triumph of the Moon: A History of Modern Pagan Witchcraft by Ronald Hutton

Western Inner Workings by William G. Gray

Witchcraft: A Tradition Renewed by Doreen Valiente and Evan John Jones

members.aol.com/akcroebuck

members.aol.com/ctubalcain

www.cyberwitch.com/bowers/
The Robert Cochrane letters to Joe Wilson, Norman and our own contribution in fond memory of Bill Gray.

www.witchvox.com/trads/trad_roebuck.html
Complete article.

ABOUT THE CONTRIBUTORS

Ann and Dave Finnin have been active in the Southern California Pagan community for 30 years. First initiated into the Mohsian Tradition in 1974, they founded the Roebuck Coven in 1976. In 1982, they traveled to England to study under Evan John Jones and were adopted into the Clan of Tubal Cain. The Roebuck became incorporated as the Ancient Keltic Church in 1989 and has initiated students in five daughter covens, located from Ventura to Riverside. The Roebuck coven is still active, teaching classes and facilitating open rituals throughout the southern California community. Dave and Ann are members of the Covenant of the Goddess and are active in Pagan Pride. They have appeared on various television shows and documentaries on Witchcraft and the Occult. They live in the San Fernando Valley.

SANTERIA/IFA
By Vinny Gaglione

A note from Trish: *While Santeria has a very long magickal history, it has only been in recent years that practitioners have really mingled with the broad-based Neo-Pagan community (at festivals, conferences, and so on). This has attracted many new followers to these two Paths. If this interests you, I strongly advocate attending an event where a recognized Santerian priest or priestess or respected representative is speaking or offering a ritual, to gather more information and insights.*

Ifa was brought to the New World from West Africa around the mid-1500s by two Babalawos (effectively, High Priests entrusted with divination), Adechima and Adiama. It is estimated to be nearly 4,000 years old and is still practiced in Nigeria. Ifa is a pre-Christian religion that was practiced throughout West Africa, with some variations according to tribes and nations.

The Fon, Dahomey, Yoruban, and Congolese all had similar religions. However, what is commonly called Ifa is practiced by the Yoruban people. It came to the Spanish and Portuguese colonies with the slaves. From there, it spread out among non-African people, to include whites and indigenous people of the islands.

Ifa's tenets encourage us to obtain a better life, both physically and spiritually, through divination, sacrifice, and ritual. Divination is used to help one find his or her way back to the Path that was determined for the individual by Olofi (God), Orunla (the secretary of God), and the individual's spirit. Orunla translates God's instructions through the Babalawo to the individual so that he may do what is necessary in order for him to improve his life.

Olofi, Olorun, and Olodumare are the three personalities of God. The Ochas/Orishas are the saints, angels, and spirits that rule the Earth. The seven main Orishas are Orunla, Ellegua, Chango, Ogun, Yemaya, Obatala, and Ochun. Many people consider Ifa polytheistic because the word *Orisha* is loosely translated as "god or goddess." However, in its purest form, it is monotheistic, because Olofi is God and the Orishas are saints/angels/Nature Spirits.

During initiations, white is the only color the Initiates can wear. Women must wear skirts that extend past their knees. All cover their heads. Once a woman is initiated, after a one-year initiation period, she may wear skirts of gingham that correspond to her Orisha.

There are many tools and altars that are used. Each Orisha has a specific altar and tools. Each Orisha also has a separate set of cowrie shells that are used for divination. Beyond this, sacred drums are an important part of many Orisha ceremonies.

Babalawos do not use the drums at their ceremonies nor are they allowed to divine with cowrie shells. Instead, the Babalawos use *Upon Ifa* (a round wooden board) and 21 *Ikines* (cola nuts) to divine for major ceremonies. Daily and less important readings are conducted with a chain of eight coconut shell medallions called *Opuele* (pronounced *oku-le*).

After spending many years studying Wicca (nearly 15) and Stregheria (an additional 10), I felt that I needed more mentoring. Santeria/Ifa has a much stronger system of mentoring and mutual support. The man that initiated me had 50 years in Ifa. My godfather, who is responsible for my training, had 30 years. My godmother had 55 years as a priestess.

The Santaria and Ifa community is very closed to outsiders. The best way to learn more is to go to a Botanica or talk to others who are in the religion. However, almost everything is very secretive.

FURTHER READING

www.religioustolerance.org/santeri.htm

ABOUT THE CONTRIBUTOR

Vinny has long been a student of many different Traditions, including the Cabala, Wicca, Stregheria, and Santeria. He first made his mark in 1988, when he opened up Spellbound Metaphysical Store, in Bloomfield, New Jersey. A small shop at first, it quickly expanded and was soon overflowing to the point that he had to rent a shop three times the original size in fewer than three years. Spellbound set the standard for what an occult shop should be by hosting many famous authors, including Scott Cunningham, Donald Michael Kraig, Ray Buckland, Trish Telesco, and so many more. It soon became apparent to all that almost all the famous authors were conducting workshops there.

Vinny developed quite a large following of his own. In 1992 he started Tempio della Stregheria, a church based on Italian Witchcraft. At the same time, he expanded by opening two additional stores, one in central New Jersey and one in North Hollywood. He also started wholesaling.

In 1995 he suffered a major heart attack and had open heart surgery. He closed down the other two stores and sold the main store. To facilitate his healing, he moved to Northeast, Pennsylvania, and opened a much smaller store in February 1998. While there, he was asked to write an astrology and magic column for several weekly newspapers.

Vinny also amazed the local radio audience with accurate readings over the air for the top radio stations in the area.

In September 1998, he was initiated into Santeria as a priest of Chango. Three months later he was initiated as a babalawo (akin to a High Priest in Wicca). This is also known as making "Ifa." He is one of the first non-Hispanic, White American babalawos—possibly the only one—in the Cuban Tradition.

As predicted in his initiation, he would have many more health problems, especially with his heart. From 2000 to 2003, he suffered six more heart attacks and had open heart surgery again in January 2003.

Currently, he still does readings, conducts ceremonies, and teaches classes throughout New Jersey, New York, and Pennsylvania. At the urging of his friends, he is currently writing books on Magick, Italian occult Traditions, and Santeria.

SEAX-WICA
By Daven

The History of Seax-Wica is a short and interesting one. There are no long myths of the origins of the Tradition, no claims to antiquity, and very few conflicting versions of how the Tradition came to be.

Seax-Wica came mainly from the vision of one man, Raymond Buckland. While he was in America teaching the Tradition he learned from Gardner to us willing Americans, he found his own ideas developing along lines that differed in important ways from Gardner's. So he kept true to his oaths of silence and split with Gardner. He spent many years researching Pagan traditions, and he sat down and wrote, from start to finish, Seax-Wica.

Seax-Wica has a basis of Saxon belief. From what Buckland has said and what I have read, there is a mish-mash of Traditions and celebrations intermixed into this Tradition, mainly because the Saxon culture itself was made up of many different Traditions as well. Many scholars have tried to separate out "pure" Saxon from the rest, and it can't be done.

Probably the best known feature of Seax-Wica is the rune script. This rune script is very close to that used by the Norse and their famous FUThARK script. Another novelty, in 1974 when Buckland started Seax-Wica, was that none of the ceremonies or rites were kept secret. There was no oath of secrecy binding members of the groups together, nor was there an iron-clad rule that stated everything learned must be passed down without any changes. Individual priests and priestesses were encouraged to do research and add to the Tradition, if it suited them, and to share that knowledge with everyone that was interested.

There are no degree systems in Seax-Wica and no initiations, other than the one that makes one a Wiccan. After that, the new Initiate has the same right and authority to speak and be heard as the priestess of the coven. From the moment of initiation, the new Wiccan is considered a priest or priestess of the gods. The actual rituals that are written down in Buckland's *The Tree* are short and to the point.

Seax-Wica is focused more on the religion of Wicca than the Witchcraft and spellcraft aspects. In *The Tree*, there is some information on spell casting, herbs, and divination, but a practitioner of Seax-Wica would be well rewarded to get some supplemental works and books on magick and divination to round out their education. This is intentional. *The Tree* assumes that the person going into Seax-Wica is either already well read in Witchcraft or they are willing to become so.

Seax-Wica, unlike most traditional groups, recognizes self-initiation. The rationale for this stance can be summed up in one phrase: "Who initiated the first Witch?" As such, the declaration of self-dedication is seen as just as valid as a coven initiation, and little to no emphasis is placed upon the lineage of a Witch. While this can and does cause some conflict with other Traditions, it also encourages those who have little to no contact with other like-minded people to acknowledge their deities and their choice of religion.

Seax-Wica is not for everyone. If you decide to follow this Tradition, there will be much asked for by the gods. Study, practice, reading and research, internalizing lessons, and evolutions of yourself will all become necessary. You will be asked to present the best of what a Wiccan priest or priestess can be, at all times, to your fellow Wiccans and to others who will never understand what Wicca is about. But despite all that, or because of it, your relationship with the gods will truly become personal and internal. This is an excellent starting point, so long as you are willing to work and do your share. And, ultimately, isn't that what a religion is supposed to do?

FURTHER READING

Buckland's Complete Book of Witchcraft by Raymond Buckland

The Tree by Raymond Buckland

geocities.com/SoHo/Workshop/6650/

groups.yahoo.com/group/seaxwica/
    A "club," if you will, similar to some other groups out there. I'm a member of this group, and I enjoy it. It's an e-mail list, and we have some good discussions there, but we are in danger of closing due to a lack of active members.

www.davensjournal.com/index.htm?SW.xhtml&2

www.seax.org/

ABOUT THE CONTRIBUTOR

Daven has been a practicing Seax-Wican since 1991, having written numerous articles about Seax-Wica for many publications. Currently he is studying Druidism, but is still involved in the Seax-Wican community online. Please visit his Web page at *www.davensjournal.com*.

STORYTELLER WICCA TRADITION: THALIA CLAN
By Dagonet Dewr, Clan Chief, Thalia Clan

The central group of the Storyteller Wicca Tradition, Thalia Clan, was founded on Beltaine 1992 CE at a campout in Burr Oak State Park in Gloucester, Ohio. At the time, the group was merely a place for celebration of friendship, family, and a mutual interest in Paganism and the occult. However, within three years, Thalia Clan was a fully functional Neo-Pagan group following a distinctive ritual framework and practice. Centered in Indianapolis, Indiana, the group and Tradition has mostly remained in the area, although individual Initiates of the Clan have moved to other locations within the United States.

Thalia Clan is an eclectic Neo-Pagan Mystery Tradition with strong Wiccan elements—a spiritual family that celebrates the seasons with joy and emphasize spiritual and emotional development through community. Ours is not a religion of dogma or creeds, but of individual faith and experience, in communion with fellow travelers on the Road, and of the Lord and Lady in all of their myriad names and forms. We explore the mysteries of Self and Deity through flexible, responsive rituals that tread the balance between mirth and reverence, and laugh in the face of darkness, for evil cannot abide mockery. Thalia is our Lady of Comedy, and Dionysus, our Lord of Dreams.

In a community that shares joy and sorrow, laughter and tears, we sing, feast, dance, make music and love, and take care of our own.

The terms *Thalia Clan* and *Storyteller Wicca* are not interchangeable. Thalia Clan is the direct and linear manifestation of the Storyteller Wicca ritual framework; the Initiates of the Clan form a central body for guidance and continued growth and evolution. Storyteller Wicca refers to the ritual framework and cosmology that Thalia and other groups have developed over the last 12 years and is still—and always—a work in progress. There are individuals who practice Storyteller Wicca without being a part of the Clan; these individuals generally value smaller-group intimacy rather than the larger extended tribal structure of Thalia Clan.

Individual working and celebratory groups within the clan are called *hearths*. Each hearth is led by two co-facilitators (usually a priest and priestess) and has other officers, called *Kinships*, who are responsible for specific facets within the hearth's functioning. The Kin to the Fire provides magical training and guidance, the Kin to the Air provides communication services and coordinates events, and the Kin to the Earth provides oracular guidance and record keeping. Most but not all hearths also refer to the priest as Kin to the Water, signifying his role as mediator and emotional support for the hearth, and the Priestess as Kin to the Center, signifying her role as gateway and guide in and into the other worlds.

Thalia does not use a traditional degree system. Instead, the Clan's internal rites of passage are called Deepening Rituals, so called "because they are experiences that deepen your connection with your gods and your clan, not something that 'raises you above' anyone else" (from the extended essay "What Is Thalia?" located at *www.geocities.com/cecylyna/thalia.html*). The first deepening, dedication, is an

affirmation of the individual's willingness to take responsibility to aid in the day-to-day operation of his or her
hearth. The second, initiation, is an affirmation of the
individual's willingness to take on the responsibility of
guiding and developing the clan as a whole. The third, the
athanor, is a recent addition to the Tradition and is an
affirmation of lifetime commitment to the gods and personal ministry, bringing the individual full-circle from the
world to a small group to a large group to the world again,
mirroring the progression of the Major Arcana of the tarot.
While individual groups may have differing requirements
for dedication, candidates for initiation must go through
specific training on both Craft-related and general pastoral
issues or provide proof of experience that makes such training superfluous. Candidates for the athanor are approved
by the High Priestess only, with input from others who
have passed through it.

Despite this, Thalia is not primarily a training tradition (although separate Storyteller Wicca groups may
change this influence). The dedication and initiation rituals
both contain Mystery elements, as do the celebrations of
the cycle of the seasons—stories and drama that are designed to illustrate central principles of the Storyteller Wicca
cosmology through experiential means. Thalia has changed
its influence to become more teaching- and knowledge-
based over the last few years, however, and as with all
things, this is a work in progress. These stories are meant
to echo tribal and pre-modern communities who passed
on history, mythology, and entertainment through
storytelling. Thalia is not, however, Reconstructuralist; the
stories told are new ones using old elements.

Clergy within Thalia have a unique role. Each hearth
has a priest and priestess; those individuals often will facilitate other working pairs or individuals within the hearth
to perform full moons or Sabbat rituals, both for training

purposes and to weave other influences and worldviews into the hearth's ritual gestalt. It is the intention of Thalia to bring every person, if not to group priesthood or priestesshood, certainly to personal priesthood/priestesshood to their own deities. Thalia values multiple pantheons and views of the gods and therefore, despite its name and patron deities, does not limit itself to the Hellenic pantheon. Current members celebrate the Welsh, Irish, Egyptian, Hellenic, and Native American mythic cycle, among others.

Thalia endorses the simple form of the Wiccan Rede, requiring candidates at both dedication and initiation to avow their continued belief that they are responsible for their own behavior and whatever they give out will come back to them. Thalia also has general guidelines for conduct and communication best summarized as "if you have something to say, say it to the person who needs to hear it" and a general policy of discouraging rumors. Many guidelines for interpersonal communication come from Amber K's *Coven Craft* and Kenneth Haugk's *Antagonists in the Church*. Thalia also has a complete ethics statement and covenant that all prospective members must swear to within the boundaries of the Circle; that statement is completely open and available for anyone to view, and is known as the Thalian Covenant.

Storyteller Wicca encourages its members who can be public activists for Pagan rights to do so. High Priestess Cecylyna Dewr and High Priest Dagonet Dewr are the President and Vice-President of the Pagan Pride Project (*www.paganpride.org*), and many other members are involved in activist causes.

While Storyteller Wicca has not been as of yet trained long-distance, truly interested parties are welcome to e-mail the High Priestess of the Storyteller Wicca Tradition, Cecylyna Dewr, or the High Priest, Dagonet Dewr.

CONTACT

E-mail: cecylyna@yahoo.com (Cecylyna Dewr)
 dagonet@paganpride.org (Dagonet Dewr)

FURTHER READING

Craft resources:
Celebrating Life by Tzipora
Devoted to You by Judy Harrow
Heart of Wicca by Ellen Cannon Reed
Invocation of the Gods by Ellen Cannon Reed
Living Wicca by Scott Cunningham
Philosophy of Wicca by Amber Laine Fisher
Spiritual Mentoring by Judy Harrow
The Spiral Dance by Starhawk
The Veil Edge by Willow Polson
Triumph of the Moon by Ronald Hutton
Wicca Covens by Judy Harrow
Witches' Bible Compleat by Janet and Stuart Farrar

Non-craft resources:
Callahan's series by Spider Robinson
Finite and Infinite Games by Richard Carse
Illusions by Richard Bach (and his other works)
Mists of Avalon by Marion Zimmer Bradley
One by Richard Bach (and his other works)
Principia Discordia (but only on Friday)
Stranger in a Strange Land by Robert Heinlein
The Road Less Traveled by M Scott Peck
Way of the Shaman by Michael Harner

ABOUT THE CONTRIBUTOR

Dagonet Dewr couldn't find a coven in the dark ages of the early 1990s, so he helped found one with a bunch of other people. Perhaps he should have known better, but since then he's had a good 12 years of on-the-job training, and thinks he's finally starting to get it right. In addition to his jobs, he's managing editor of *newWitch* magazine (for more information see *www.newwitch.com*) and a doting father of three kids and one guinea pig. He enjoys cooking, baseball, writing music reviews, and gaming.

TEMPLE OF ARA (ARA TRADITION)
By Ally Peltier

The Ara Tradition was founded in 1983, with the birth of the Circle of Ara, led by High Priestess Phyllis Curott. Ara is a nondogmatic, innovative, and progressive Wiccan Tradition that traces its roots to the Minoan and Gardnerian traditions in New York City. At the same time that she was training in the Minoan Sisterhood, Phyllis was studying core Shamanism and actively participating in the first Shamanic drumming circle based on the work of Dr. Michael Harner. As High Priestess of the Circle of Ara, now one of the oldest and longest-running Wiccan congregations in the United States, Phyllis deconstructed traditional and often patriarchal Wiccan teachings to distill a system of core practices and principles, then blended these with core Shamanic practices.

It is this model of teachings, referred to as Core Shamanic Wicca, that she has passed on to her students. After numerous daughter and granddaughter circles, lectures, workshops, and books, Curott and the Elders realized that their Tradition had grown and evolved into an international movement, and so the Temple of Ara was formed, in order to formalize and maintain the Ara Tradition across the globe.

Ara is based on the central principle and experience of immanent divinity. It reflects years of Shamanic Wiccan practice and is intended to help us discover the Divine that dwells within and all around us and to rejoice in the ecstasy of that communion. We experience the interconnectedness between all things on this Earth, acknowledging that each is part of a greater whole and that each is inherently sacred. We celebrate the natural cycles of birth, growth, death, and rebirth and practice rites that attune ourselves with the natural cycles of the Earth, including the lunar and solar cycles. Ara Witches celebrate the equality of the female and male, which is manifest in all things, including the Divine—known to us as the Goddess and the God.

Because we celebrate the erotic and ecstatic dance between Goddess and God, Ara Witches value consensual sex as a source of pleasure and sacred communion, and the act that brings about all creation. Ara Witches regularly practice magic, which we define as "a dynamic process by which [we] co-create reality with Deity," and engage in dialogue with the Divine, using various tools for divination. We also acknowledge the right and responsibility of all individuals to take charge of their own spiritual development and to do what they will with their own bodies, as long as they do not inflict harm on themselves or others nor infringe on the rights of others, and we encourage tolerance for all beings, regardless of race, gender, sexual preference, lifestyle choice, religion, or species.

We acknowledge the existence of realities far greater than those apparent to everyday perception. We know that, through ritual and other Wiccan practices, we experience those realities and thus gain wisdom. We acknowledge and experience Nature and the Earth as an embodiment or expression of the Divine, and so the natural world is treated with reverence and respect. For Ara Witches, Nature is the greatest of all spiritual teachers, and so we seek not only to live in harmony with the Earth, but to actively spend time in wilderness and other natural environments as a source of wisdom and spiritual transformation.

The Temple of Ara does not acknowledge the existence of an absolute evil, but we acknowledge that human beings commit cruel or "evil" acts when they become disconnected from the Sacred or Divine. The core ethical precept of the Temple of Ara is: We seek to live in a sacred manner because we live in a sacred world. The Temple of Ara does not have "rules" for practicing Witchcraft and magic. Ara Witches do not subscribe to the "Threefold Law"—whatever you send out magically will come back to you threefold—because it is a rule based upon punishment and fear and, as such, is not a true ethical precept. Witches in the Temple of Ara do not harm, use baneful magic, or use magic to manipulate others, because we recognize the Divine in all things and strive to act in accord with this philosophy by treating all with reverence, respect, compassion, and gratitude.

CONSULTING AN ORACLE

Feeling that daily communing with the Divine is paramount, this exercise is intended to help one see more clearly, specifically with regard to yourself. Recommended media include runes, tarot, or the I Ching. Begin by grounding and centering. Honor and invite the Divine to communicate with you. Hold your oracle to your heart and state your purpose. Then, look at the oracle and receive your message. Meditate on the information you're given, being sure to write it down. After you've recorded your impressions, you may refer to your oracle's guidebook for further interpretations. Remember, seeing your shadows, and acknowledging them, is a critical first step in integrating and transforming them. If you have been shown a shadow side of yourself, ask the oracle what you need to understand and what you need to do to transform the negative with which you have been living into what is positive and best for you. Thank the oracle and the Divine for the advice. Internalize what you've been given and honor it by putting it into action in your life.

CONTACT

Website: *www.templeofara.org*
E-mail: Info@templeofara.org

FURTHER READING

Book of Shadows by Phyllis Curott
The Love Spell by Phyllis Curott
    Forthcoming from Gotham Books in February 2005.
Witch Crafting by Phyllis Curott
groups.yahoo.com/group/AraNews
    Visit this site to join the Ara News electronic announcement list.

ABOUT THE CONTRIBUTOR

Ally Peltier is an Elder of the Ara Tradition and serves on the Temple of Ara's Board of Directors and Council of Elders. She is currently the editor-in-chief of the "Ara Quarterly" newsletter and has also served for several years as the assistant editor of *Cauldrons and Broomsticks* e-zine. She has contributed to *Pop! Goes the Witch* and *The Coven* by Fiona Horne and has had numerous articles appear in *Circle Magazine*, *Cauldrons and Broomsticks* e-zine, and other non-Pagan venues. Ally, who has also written under the name Brenna Fey, lives in New York City.

TRADITIONAL BRITISH DRUIDRY (TBD)
By John Michael Greer

The original Druids were the priests and philosophers of the ancient Celtic peoples of Britain, Ireland, Gaul, and other areas settled during the great Celtic invasions of the first millennium BCE. Very little is actually known about them, their teachings, or their practices, as Druidry in its original form was essentially extinct by 750 CE.

Efforts to revive the Druidic teachings were apparently being made in Wales as early as the high Middle Ages, judging by traces in Welsh bardic literature of the time. It was not until the Renaissance, though, that the first stirrings of what is now Traditional British Druidry (TBD) began to take shape. Many Renaissance thinkers sought what was called the *prisca theologia* or "primal theology"—a revelation of the truth of things which had been given to humanity in the earliest times and might be recovered by studying and working with the remnants of ancient spiritual and magical Traditions.

William Stukeley (1629–1697) was a major figure in this revival. He was the first scholar since ancient times to make a serious study of Stonehenge and other megalithic monuments, and Tradition has it that he refounded the Mount Haemus grove at Oxford in 1694. In 1717, according to Tradition, Stukeley's friend and student John Toland

(1670–1722) founded a Druid organization in London, from which most groups in Traditional British Druidry trace their descent.

In the latter part of the 19th century, Druidry was profoundly influenced by the contemporary occult revival launched by Eliphas Levi (1801–1875) and popularized around the world by the Theosophical Society from 1875 on. Existing Druid rituals and practices were reshaped and expanded in the light of the wider Western occult Tradition during these years. In the years after 1900, the collapse of the Hermetic Order of the Golden Dawn—the most influential English magical order—brought many capable occultists into Druid orders, where they shared their knowledge freely.

Modernly, different Druid orders have different approaches to Druidry, and attempts to hammer out a common code of beliefs have rarely gotten far. What unites Traditional British Druidry is a reverence for the lore and legend of the ancient Druids and a commitment to Traditions of knowledge and practice evolved over the years since the Druid revival of the 17th century, not adherence to a particular creed. Still, some elements of belief are common to most traditional Druids.

Many traditional Druids and Druid orders are comfortable with monotheistic ideas of the Divine to an extent that startles most other Pagans. While it's by no means universal, and there are polytheistic and Goddess-oriented currents in Traditional British Druidry, the word *God* (or its synonyms in Welsh and other Celtic languages) gets used surprisingly often.

Druids believe in reincarnation and the soul's evolution. Every soul must experience every form of life, from the simplest one-celled organism to the most complex and intelligent animal and plant forms, "doing all and suffering all" in the course of its pilgrimage. Reaching the human level at last, each soul has the chance to make the leap to Gwynfydd, the enlightened life, or to fail and fall back. This perspective gives Traditional British Druidry a deep reverence for life in all forms, and an essentially optimistic view of the possibilities for good in all beings.

Sacred Geometry and Geomancy are both strongly integrated into TBD. Since the first days of the 17th-century Druid renaissance, these have been a major focus of study and speculation. Similarly, legends of King Arthur and the knights and ladies of his court have been a major resource for Traditional British Druidry for centuries. Through these stories, important spiritual teachings are found, and can be understood and applied through study and meditation.

As with most Pagan Traditions, Traditional British Druidry consists of a free mix of groups and solitary prac-titioners. Groups, called *groves*, are headed by a Chief, Chief Druid, or Archdruid (who may be of either gender), and have a wide range of structures—from the relatively informal circle around a teacher, on the one hand, to large orders with a complex structure derived from fraternal lodge sources, on the other. Some groves trace their an-cestry back to John Toland's London Grove in 1717, while others are of more recent vintage.

Welsh and Irish bardic lore set TBD's ethical stan-dards. The maintenance of peace is an essential standard of conduct; the ancient Druids were famed for their power to part armies on the verge of battle and bring about a peaceful settlement to the quarrel. To this day, in most Druid ceremonies, the presiding Druid must proclaim peace to the four quarters before any other action can take place.

The ethical principles of Druidry are founded on what modern philosophers call *virtue ethics*—that is, virtues such as courage, honesty, and fairness form the standards which

Druids strive to follow, and those who make a habit of willfully violating these standards are unlikely to be welcome in Druid groves. Outside its ethical principles, Druidry has no particular requirements (in terms of daily behavior), no taboos to avoid, and no observances to enforce. The exercise of virtue in everyday life, the studies and spiritual practices of the Druid Tradition, and the celebrations of the Druid year make up the life of Traditional British Druidry.

The Universal Druid Prayer

Grant, O God, Thy protection;

And in protection, strength;

And in strength, understanding;

And in understanding, knowledge;

And in knowledge, the knowledge of justice;

And in the knowledge of justice, the love of it;

And in that love, the love of all existences;

*And in the love of all existences,
the love of God and all goodness.*

Most systems of Traditional British Druidry also include a selection of personal spiritual disciplines for the use of members. These vary widely, but certain forms of meditation are much practiced, and energy work devoted to formulating and energizing the Body of Light is also common. These are less colorful but at least as important as the public ceremonies, because as a wisdom Tradition, Druidry has as a major focus on the spiritual development of its Initiates.

A resource worth mentioning is the postal course in Druidry offered by the Order of Bards Ovates and Druids (OBOD). While OBOD's current approach combines elements of Traditional British Druidry with much that's drawn from the modern Pagan revival, it's probably the best available starting point for anyone seriously interested in Traditional British Druidry—even aside from its value on its own terms, which is considerable. The course covers the three grades of Bard, Ovate, and Druid, and takes at least three years to complete. For more information, contact the OBOD.

CONTACT

Website: *www.druidry.org*
E-mail: threelynx@earthlink.net (John Michael Greer)
Address: The Order of Bards Ovates and Druids
    PO Box 1333
    Lewes, E. Sussex, BN7 1DX, England

FURTHER READING

The Bardic Sourcebook, edited by John Matthews
    A resource worth using, this is part of a trilogy of sourcebooks edited by Matthews. The trilogy contains a great deal of information from old documents and out-of-print sources, including some substantial selections from the writings of Iolo Morganwg.
The Book of Druidry by Ross Nichols
    A thorough book on the subject. Nichols was the guiding spirit behind the foundation of OBOD, and his work is deeply informed by a long background in Traditional British Druidry. A good comparison to the newer approaches in Philip Carr-Gomm's *The Druid Way*.

The Celtic Seers Sourcebook, edited by John Matthews
   Part of a trilogy of sourcebooks edited by Matthews.

The Druid Sourcebook, edited by John Matthews
   Part of a trilogy of sourcebooks edited by Matthews.

The Druid Way by Philip Carr-Gomm
   Philip Carr-Gomm is the OBOD's current Chosen
   Chief. This excellent text, when compared to *The
   Book of Druidry* by Ross Nichols, gives a good sense
   of the differences between the older approach (in
   Nichols's book) and the work now being done by
   OBOD.

The Earth Spirit by John Michell
   A work permeated by the traditional Druid outlook
   of John Michell, this book is well worth careful
   study by the student of Traditional British Druidry

The Magic Arts in Celtic Britain by Lewis Spence
   Perhaps the best of the older books, although shaped
   by Spence's Theosophical approach.

The New View Over Atlantis by John Michell
   Another of Mitchell's works well worth studying.

www.witchvox.com/trads/trad_traddruidry.html

ABOUT THE CONTRIBUTOR

   John Michael Greer has been a student of Hermetic
magic and the Western occult Traditions for 25 years and
is the author of several books on magic, divination, and
occult philosophy. He is also a Druid of the Order of Bards
Ovates and Druids (OBOD), serves on the Council of
Archdruids of the ancient Order of Druids in America,
and is a student of Traditional British Druidry. He can be
reached at mezla@hotmail.com.

TRADITIONAL TANTRIC TRADITION
By Shambhalanath
(aka Donald Michael Kraig)

A note from Trish: *Donald was among the first of the "big-name Pagans" I ever had the privilege to get to know. He immediately dismantled the notion that such celebrities were uppity or egocentric with his unique genuineness and great sense of humor. He may not remember that event, but it was one in which Don also offered this fledgling author very sound advice and insights, for which I am incredibly grateful.*

Tantra? Do you mean that sex stuff? The popular awareness in the West of Tantra began with the writings of Sir John Woodroffe (using the name Arthur Avalon) during the British Victorian Age. There was a great deal of sexual repression during that period, and the only way it was popularly safe to discuss sexuality was when it was related to other cultures. Since Woodroffe's books did discuss sexuality, it was almost inevitable that sex would be the prurient focus of the Victorians. But to say that Tantra is about sex is like saying that Wicca is primarily about the Great Rite.

Tantra may be the oldest magical Tradition in continuous development and practice. Its origins go back to the Harrapan culture of the Indus Valley (modern Kashmir), at least 5,000 years ago. This culture, which may go back 10,000 years or more, was centered on the Saraswati river, and one city was almost equal in population to the entire population of Egypt. The civilization vanished at about the time the Saraswati dried up, but the people went south into modern India, east to China, and even northwest into Europe. At least one author claims that these people made valuable contributions to the birth of Druidism and Witchcraft.

In India, the teachings of these people evolved in many ways including to the many Paths of what is collectively known as Tantra. Virtually all metaphysical concepts that are considered "Hindu," are actually Tantric. This includes such things as chakras, kundalini, and much more. Acupuncture, acupressure, martial arts, feng shui, karma, mantra, breathwork and energywork, advanced mathematics, and even astrology, often attributed to others, began with the ancient Tantrics (although they often evolved and advanced elsewhere).

Today, Tantra is frowned upon in most of India, even though the major spiritual systems of that land, collectively called Hinduism, borrowed many concepts from Tantra. This is similar to the way Christianity has borrowed many ideas from Pagan Traditions. In the West, there are two major trends in Tantra, Neo-Tantra (as popularized by Osho aka Rajneesh), which tends to focus on sexual energy, and Traditional Tantra which is a complete spiritual system.

Tantric spirituality focuses on a God and Goddess, Shiva and Shakti. Some groups focus on one over the other. Shiva and Shakti are often seen as manifestations of a transcendent deity, and Tantrics often work with numerous deities (primarily goddesses) who can be seen as aspects of the deity. In Tantra, the male is seen as passive and the female is seen as active, the exact opposite of Western Traditions.

There are also 10 Wisdom Goddesses (the Dasa Mahavidyas) who could be related to the Tree of Life, although Tantrics use numerous symbolic forms known as *yantras*. The most sacred, the sri yantra, is actually worshiped by some people. It functions like the Kabalistic Tree of Life but is far more complex.

Other deities include Agni, the deity of fire; Durga, the main appearance of Shakti, which represents the combined powers of all the deities; and Ganesh, the breaker of obstacles. Ganesh also functions much like Thoth or Mercury. Kali, a manifestation of Shakti, is the loving goddess of destruction (of all that is unwanted).

As with other Traditions, Tantrics have a set of yearly festivals. These do not traditionally have set dates as Tantrics work with a lunar calendar. The festivals are associated with the equinoxes and solstices, major deities, and the birthday of each individual Tradition's leader or guru. Some can be very solemn and others quite rowdy.

Tantric Traditions have daily rituals, as well as ones for personal events (births, deaths, weddings, and so on). There are also devotional rituals to the deities. Rituals are collectively known as *pujas*, and can run from the very mundane to the extremely sexual, as in the puja described in the book *The Yoni Tantra*, where a woman is honored as the Goddess. The ritual known as the Rite of the Five Ms, ending with spiritualized intercourse, has been frequently described.

As a complete spiritual system that is legitimately thousands of years old, it would require a book to describe some of the most basic beliefs. Some of them include:

▶ *Sahaja*: This is the idea that we have moved away from a condition of naturalness and a goal is to return to a natural way of life. When you are in a state of naturalness, you live in the present moment. When it comes to sexuality, the focus on orgasm is looking at the future. By focusing on the feelings of the present moment you can lengthen the period of sexual activity, resulting in the fame of Tantric lovers.

▶ *Svecchacharya*: This is key concept for many Tantrics, as it means "the path of finding one's will and doing it."

▶ *Maya*: One of the most positive and interesting beliefs of many Tantrics is that, unlike numerous other Traditions that see the world as horrible (Hinduism, Christianity, some forms of Buddhism, for example), Tantrics view the world as a wonderful place to spiritually evolve. We don't see this as true because we are caught in the illusion of maya. This is also known as the dance of the goddess Maya, which is so beautiful and enticing that we see the dance instead of the goddess. Similarly, maya prevents us from seeing the beauty of the physical world or thinking that it is different from the magnificence of the non-physical worlds. Maya is caused by the kleshas.

▶ *Kleshas*: The kleshas are five blockages to enlightenment. They are Avidya (Ignorance) of the reality of the universe; Asmita (Ego), a false sense of who and what you are; Raga (Attachment), desiring to possess physical things as they end up controlling you; Dvesha (Repulsion), the lack of understanding that nothing is horrible save that we make it so; and Abhinivesha (Clinging to Life), avoiding living life to its fullest due to fear of death.

▶ *Reincarnation and karma*: Karma is a natural law that the universe responds to your actions, not your motivations. It is the law of cause and effect. It may take many lifetimes for you to work through your karma. It should be noted that karma is neither positive nor negative; it simply is. The purpose of karma is to teach you about what you need to learn to spiritually develop. Karma corresponds to the Wiccan Threefold Law.

▶ *Non-physical bodies*: We have non-physical bodies or sheaths (*koshas*). Spiritual energy moves in and out of the bodies through vortices called *chakras*. There are hundreds of chakras, and different traditions focus on three, six, seven, or more major ones. Spiritual development can take place via movement of the kundalini energy through the chakras.

▶ *Right- and left-hand Paths*: In Western Traditions, this generally refers to positive or negative systems. This is not true in Tantra, where a right-hand Path is mental while the left-hand path is physical. Both are considered valid.

▶ *Kundalini*: This is the mental/physical energy of the spiritual and physical bodies. Those on the right-hand Path try to raise this energy using breathwork and visualization in order to achieve a state of enlightenment. This process is called *laya yoga*, although in the West it is commonly referred to as *kundalini yoga*. It can take years of practice to achieve success, if at all. Left-hand Tantric practices use a combination of spiritualized sexuality, breathwork, visualization, and mantra to achieve the goal much more quickly.

▶ *Magick*: Includes both folk magick and ceremonial magick, including sex magick.

FURTHER READING:

A Chakra and Kundalini Workbook by Jonn Mumford
Chakras by Harish Johari
In Search of the Cradle of Civilization by Georg Feuerstein, David Frawley, and Subhash Kak

Mahanirvana Tantra by Arthur Avalon
Origins of Modern Witchcraft by Ann Moura
Tantra by Georg Feuerstein
The Serpent Power by Arthur Avalon
Tools for Tantra by Harish Johari
Wheels of Life by Anodea Judith
www.shivashakti.com/

ABOUT THE CONTRIBUTOR

Shambhalanath (Donald Michael Kraig) is an internationally known author, lecturer, and writer. He has been initiated into three Tantric systems, including that of AMOOKOS (the Arcane and Magickal Order of the Knights of Shambhala), part of the 1,000-year-old Nath Tantric Traditionwhere he was given the name Shambhalanath (Lord of Shambhala). He has also been initiated into Tantric Kriya Yoga and NAMASTE (New Association of MAgical, Sexual and Tantric Explorers) and has studied with many instructors. His books include *Modern Magick*, *Modern Sex Magick*, and *Tarot and Magic*.

WITCHCRAFT
By Trish Telesco

This section is dedicated to basic Witchcraft, not Wicca the religion. Magick and the arts of a Witch need not be practiced in a philosophical or religious construct. In this case, the methods and tools are utilized as means of helping the Witch accomplish specific goals. Without the dogmatic construct, the compass that guides how a Witch uses energy ultimately resides in his or her heart.

The history of magickal arts, as a whole, is very long and tangled. They extend into every culture and era imaginable.

As early civilizations grew and flourished, humankind's curiosity naturally grew as well. Among the common strands of thought that emerged was that life is connected and there is more to it than meets the eye. So people tried to find ways to influence life's web, either to change things or to understand what could not be seen. Those methods that appeared to work were repeated. The repeats that also worked were consigned to Tradition!

The people who learned these arts bore many names, including Shaman, Wise Person, and of course, Witch. It is not until around the 1300s, however, that we find substantial writings about Witches, most of them being of a negative connotation, thanks to the Witch hunts. From what we can gather, however, Witchcraft as we now know it blended many practices and customs that mixed and mingled through trade routes and war. Paganism, Hebrew mysticism and Roman and Greek mythology all had a hand in what remains with us today.

The last recorded execution of a Witch occurred in Germany in 1775, and the sad reality is that the person involved may not have even been practicing magickal arts at all. Many of the Witch hunts were driven by fear and profit-mongering. Thankfully, with the 1800s, a new, more thoughtful attitude developed on the heels of a rapidly changing world. Witchcraft began to be seen as a nature religion, and public interest in occult arts increased. In the next 100 years, the new breed of Witch would rise from the ashes into modern controversy.

By the 1970s, the revival of "old ways" was rolling along with ever-increasing energy. People were interested in the art of magick, and particularly in psychic phenomena. There were several schools of Witchery in practice, and the Wiccan religion was growing in popularity. However, among those interested in the Craft were those who stuck to more of a hearth-and-home, folkways approach. They chose to stay simply Witches, not Wiccans or Pagans, even though they share many similarities in practice and ideals to both groups.

I would also hazard to say that a large majority of Witches are solitary practitioners, which has been the way since early days. Consequently, the basics of belief and practice remain quite unique. It's fairly safe to say that all honor nature, all have a reverence for life, and many enjoy herbal and related arts because of how easily they tie-into magickal Arts. To learn more about Witches, you can read dozens of books, or you can just ask one—ask 10!

CONTACT

Website: *www.loresinger.com*
　　Trish Telesco's home page.

INDEX

A

Adventure Wicca, 41-44

Alexandrian Tradition, 44-49

animal guide/totem, finding a, 127

Appalachian Folk Magick, 49-52

Aquarian Tabernacle Church, 52-56

Ár nDraíocht Féin, 56-61

Arician Tradition, 62-66

Asatru, 66-71

Avalon Tradition, 71-77

B

binding sinful habits, 97-98

Blue Star Wicca, 77-81

British Druid Order, 81-85

C

Celtic Reconstructionist Paganism, 85-89

Central Valley Wicca: Kingstone Tradition, 89-94

changing Paths, 31-32

Charge of Eris, 120-121

Christian Witchcraft, 94-98

Church of All Worlds, 98-102

Circle Craft, 103-106

consulting an oracle, 234-235

Correllian Nativist Tradition, 106-109

Covenant of Unitarian Universalist Pagans, 109-111

covens, 23

Cybeline, 111-113

Dianic Tradition, 114-118

Discordianism-Erisianism, 119-123

Eclectic Wicca and Paganism, 123-128

Esoteric Catholic/Cherokee, 128-131

F

Faerie Faith, 131-133

Feri Tradition: Vicia Line, 134-137

finding
    a Path, 27-30
    an animal guide/totem, 127

Finding Spell, 24

Fool, the, 17-19

Full Moon poem, 203

Gardnerian Tradition, 137-141

Georgian Tradition, 141-146

Golden Dawn, 146-148

Green Witchcraft, 149-153

group practice, finding, 24

group, warnings when looking for a, 25-26

Gwyddonic Order, 153-156

Haitian Vodou: Serving the Spirits, 156-161

Heathen (Germanic Paganism), 161-164

Hellenism (Hellenic Ethnic Tradition), 164-166

Holy Order of Mother Earth (HOME), 166-169

K

Keltrian Druidism, 170-174

Kitchen Witch ABCs, 175-176

Kitchen Witchcraft, 174-177

M

Mahlorian Green Craft: A Mystery Fayerie Tradition, 177-180

Manifesto of the Georgians, 144-145

Maypole "Instructions," 43

Mi'nerwen Tradition, 180-184

Minoan Tradition, 184-187

Mixed Gender Dianic Wicca, 187-190

mixing Traditions, 13

Mohsian Tradition, 190-194

New Age religions, early texts dealing with, 12

New England Covens of Traditionalist Witches (NECTW), 194-198

New York Welsh Tradition, 198-201

Oak and Stone Path, 201-204

Ophidian Traditional Witchcraft, 204-209

oracle, consulting an, 234-235

Path,
    finding a, 27-30
    changing, 31-32

Paths and practices, 21-32

RavenMyst Circle, 209-212

Reclaiming Tradition Witchcraft, 212-216

Rede of the Wiccae, 195-196

Roebuck Tradition, 217-221

sample love ritual, 125

Santeria/Ifa, 221-224

Seax-Wica, 224-227

sects, different Wiccan and Neo-Pagan, 12-13

"1734" Tradition, 37-41

solitary or group practice, 21-27

solitary practice,
    advantages of, 21-23
    disadvantages of, 23-24

Solstice Spell for Consecration, 129-130

spell for finding a group, 24

Storyteller Wicca Tradition: Thalia Clan, 227-232

Temple of Ara (Ara Tradition), 232-236

Tradition, choosing a, 11-13

Traditional British Druidry, 236-241

Traditional Tantric Tradition, 242-247

Traditions, mixing, 13

Universal Druid Prayer, The, 239

Witchcraft, 247-249

ABOUT TRISH TELESCO

Trish Telesco is a mother of three, wife, chief human to five pets, and a full-time professional author with numerous books on the market. These include the best-selling *Exploring Candle Magick, Money Magick, Gardening With the Goddess, A Witch's Beverages and Brews, An Enchanted Life, Kitchen Witch's Guide to Divination* and other diverse titles, each of which represents a different area of spiritual interest for her and her readers.

Trish considers herself a down-to-earth Kitchen Witch whose love of folklore and worldwide customs flavor every one of her spells and rituals. Originally self-trained and self-initiated in Wicca, she later received initiation into the Strega tradition of Italy, which gives form and fullness to the folk magick Trish practices. Her strongest beliefs lie in following personal vision, being tolerant of other traditions, making life an act of worship, and being creative so that magick grows with you.

Trish travels at least twice a month to give lectures and workshops around the country on Neo-Paganism,

Wicca, Folk Magick, and many other spiritual topics. She has appeared on several television segments including *Sightings*, on mulicultural divination systems, and *National Geographic Today–Solstice Celebrations*. All the while, she maintains a strong, visible presence in metaphysical journals including Circle Network News, and on the Internet through popular sites such as *www.witchvox.com* (festival focus); her interactive home page, *www.loresinger.com*; and Yahoo club, *groups.yahoo.com/groups/folkmagicwithtrishtelesco*; and various appearances on Internet chats and bbs boards.

Her hobbies include gardening, herbalism, brewing, singing, hand crafts, antique restoration, and landscaping. Her current project is helping support various Neo-Pagan causes, including land funds for religious retreats.